The **Fabric &**
Yarn Dyer's Handbook

The **Fabric &**
Yarn Dyer's
Handbook

TRACY KENDALL

C&B
COLLINS & BROWN

For Jamie and Charlie

First published in Great Britain in 2001 by
Collins & Brown Limited
London House, Great Eastern Wharf,
Parkgate Road, London SW11 4NQ

1 2 3 4 5 6 7 8 9

British Library Cataloguing-in-Publication Data:
A catalogue record for this book is available from
the British Library

ISBN 1-85585-879-7

Project Editor **Hilary Sagar**
Art direction and design **Ruth Hope**
Photography **Tino Tedaldi**
Editorial Assistant **Niamh Hatton**
Reproduction by **Classic Scan Pte Ltd., Singapore**
Printed and bound in **Singapore by Tat Wei**

Distributed in the United States and Canada by Sterling Publishing Co,
387 Park Avenue South, New York, NY 10016,USA

Owing to the limitations of colour printing, expect some variation between
the printed page and your own dyed textiles. Other factors will influence the
final result, including: type of fabric used, age of natural dye product,
variation of time, amount of dye used etc.

**Always handle poisonous and corrosive chemicals with care. Follow
the manufacturer's instructions; store chemicals in a secure place, out
of the reach of children and in clearly marked, non-food containers.**

Information advice and statements made in this book with regard to methods
and techniques are believed to be true and accurate. however, neither the
author, copyright holder nor publisher can accept legal liability for omissions.

contents

Above A panel of devoréd velvet is used to cover a simple dining chair to create a luxurious seat.

Below Marbled fabric can be used on its own or as creative inspiration for other fabrics.

Foreword

D yeing and decorating fabric and yarn is a constantly challenging experience. Each time a new piece of work is undertaken, an amazing variety of combinations and possibilities immediately confronts you. Sometimes when working on fabrics for myself or for other designers there are very specific require-ments – about colour, design and scale, as well as about the textile and whether it is for use in fashion or interiors

These projects have often been challenging. I have had to dye lengths of silk to match the colour of a perfume and to recreate repeating designs from fragments of ancient pottery to print on the edges of a skirt. But every challenge added to my experience, and with perseverance, and some trial and error, the desired result was achieved.

Other assignments have allowed more freedom. These range from painting Patrick Caulfield-inspired designs onto jeans for high-fashion catwalk shows to designing fabric for cushion covers to fit in with my own interior.

The fabrics or yarns that you choose to dye and decorate can have the same variety of purpose. By following the recipes and techniques explained in this book you can cross dye and print your own chair covers, refresh a tired T-shirt with a simple tie-dye recipe or knit a garment in your own customized shades.

After 15 years of dealing with textiles on a day-to-day basis I am still able to enjoy putting a familiar design on a new fabric, or in a new colourway, refreshing both myself and the design in the process.

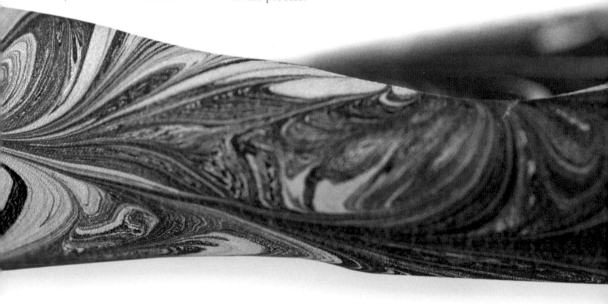

Experience has taught me always to persevere. Even if the fabric doesn't turn out as you had planned, it can often be a pleasant surprise, or at least a lesson learned. There are so many variables when dealing with textiles and yarns and often not all of them are within your control. Sometimes it is best simply to experiment and see what you can achieve with these amazing techniques and recipes.

Enjoy!

Tracy Kendall

Above A simple salt technique on silk creates an unusual fabric for either clothing or to use in home embellishments.

Left Printing an oversized feather design on sheer silk organza with easy-to-use pigment dye colour creates an unusual table runner. Sometimes a simple idea can create the most stunning fabric for interior decorating.

introduction

This section gets you started. You'll learn how to test fabrics and yarns, so you can tell which suits which dye process best. It explains how to prepare your textiles and describes the basic tools and materials you will need, as well as detailing the natural and synthetic dyes available. There are also useful hints on choosing designs and using colour effectively.

Identifying fabrics

The simplest way to identify a piece of fabric is by the way it feels and handles, and by noting how it looks. To be sure of your fabric you can try buying from a supplier of specific textiles, such as a silk manufacturer.

The touch of silk is usually smooth and soft; wool is warm to the touch; viscose can feel cold; nylon is often stiff; linen and cotton are cool and crisp and polyester is smooth and can be slightly rigid. If you are uncertain what type of fabric you have bought, a simple burn test will help you to identify it. All the indicators to look out for during the burn test are listed in the chart on page 19. Once you have identified your fabric, you will be able to choose an appropriate recipe to colour or decorate your fabric with confidence.

The recipes in this book cover the eight main types of fabric and the hundreds of variations in fabric structure and weight within these categories. For example, silk can range from the finest chiffon to upholstery-weight fabric; while wool can vary from lightweight scarf fabric to heavy blanket material.

Fabrics are normally identified by their fibre content and type and these break down as:

Natural fibres Cellulose (from plants) – cotton, linen, hemp, ramie, sisal, jute and pineapple. Protein (from animals) – silk, wool, cashmere, mohair, angora and camel.

Synthetic fibres Nylon, viscose, polyester, acrylic, elastane, polypropylene, polyethylene, Tencel, rubber, Modal, cellulose acetate and cellulose triacetate.

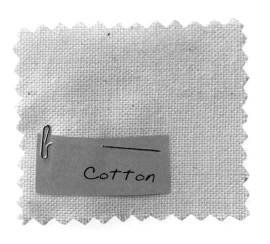

Cotton

A cellulose fabric obtained from the fibrous substance of the cotton plant, *Gossypium*. It can range from fine organdie to heavy canvas. It absorbs water easily and can take high temperatures, making dyeing easier.

Linen

The oldest known fabric, with examples found dating back to 6000BC, linen is produced from the flax plant, *Linum usitatissimum*. Although it is a cellulose fabric, it takes time to absorb dye, but is extremely durable.

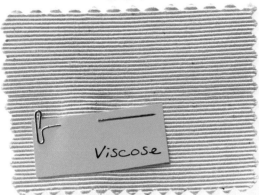

Silk

The silkworm, the caterpillar of the moth *Bombyx mori*, spins a smooth silk thread. This can be woven into different qualities and weights of silk fabrics. These accept dye easily, producing intense, vibrant colours.

Wool

Wool is obtained from various breeds of sheep and goats. This protein fibre produces a warm, flexible fabric that absorbs dye easily. As it is sensitive to high temperatures, wash it carefully during processing.

Nylon

Nylon or polyamide absorbs dye well. Developed by American chemist Wallace H. Carothers in 1935, it was the first stretch fabric. Its most famous form was as nylon stockings in the 1940s and 1950s.

Viscose

Viscose is used extensively in the fashion industry. It was invented in 1892 and is produced by breaking down wood pulp with a strong alkali. It absorbs dye well and evenly, producing intense, vivid colours.

Polyester

This synthetic fibre was developed in Britain by ICI in 1941. It is very strong but requires a high temperature to absorb dye. Now made from recycled plastics, it is mixed with natural fibres to produce a wide range of textiles.

Mixed fibres

Many fabrics are produced from a mixture of fibres, the combinations depending on the purpose it will be used for. A classic example is devoré velvet, which weaves together silk and viscose fibre to produce the most luxurious of cloths.

Cotton

Cotton is a natural cellulose fabric obtained from the fibrous substance of the cotton plant, *Gossypium*. It is an extremely versatile fabric that has been woven, dyed and decorated throughout the world for thousands of years.

There are many different types of cotton and it is therefore suitable for a wide range of uses. Fine cotton is used for baby clothes and everyday clothing for millions of people, and thick cotton is a useful fabric for chair coverings, curtains and even camping tents. Able to withstand high temperatures, yet soft and absorbent, cotton is an ideal fabric for dyeing and decorating with either natural or synthetic dyes.

The range of plain cotton fabrics available for the home dyer or decorator is enormous – try experimenting with fine, thick, coarse, textured, stiff, soft and even recycled cotton.

- **Dyes** Cold-water reactive and hot-water reactive, direct dyes, natural dyes.
- **Techniques** Tie-dyeing (page 42), batik (page 44), screenprinting (page 50).
- **Cotton recipes** Indigo (page 72), cutch on cotton (page 92).

Linen

Linen is the oldest known natural cellulose fibre, with examples found at Catal Huyuk in Turkey dating from 6000BC. Produced from the flax plant, *Linum usitatissimum*, which gives it its cream colour, it is a very durable fibre. Linen can be woven to provide both cool summer-clothing-weight fabric and hardwearing furnishing fabrics. It does not absorb water as well or as readily as other fabrics, but once fully wet, you can dye and decorate it with the same natural and synthetic dyes used for cotton fabrics.

Linen is often mixed with other fibres to reduce its tendency to crease. A good source of linen for the craft dyer and decorator is old linen bed sheets which are luxuriously soft because linen improves with age and washing.

- **Dyes** Direct dyes, hot- and cold-water reactive dyes. Natural dyes such as indigo and cutch can also be used.
- **Techniques** Screenprinting (page 50), mono-printing (page 52), batik (page 44), tie-dyeing (page 42).
- **Linen recipes** Indigo (page 72), tea time (page 87). cutch on cotton (page 92).

Silk

Silk is a natural protein fabric obtained from the silkworm, the caterpillar of the moth *Bombyx mori*. Silk is mainly produced in China and Japan, where it is patterned with specialized resist techniques such as shibori (see page 70). Cultivated silkworms are fed on a diet of

mulberry leaves, but wild silkworms that produce wild silk, also known as tussah silk or Shantung silk, feed on oak leaves. Wild silk is not as smooth and even in appearance as the cultivated silk, but it has its own qualities, charms and uses. When dyed and decorated, silk is able to pick up the most vibrant and intense colours. It can be decorated easily at home and can be used in a variety of ways. Whether dyed or decorated, silk is mostly used for clothing and is often associated with luxury items. Silk also possesses the useful quality of being cool on the skin in summer and warm in the winter.

- **Dyes** Acid dyes, reactive dyes, natural dyes.
- **Techniques** Colour stripping (page 58).
- **Silk recipes** One-colour shading (page 102), gingko silk (page 113).

Wool

Wool is a natural protein fibre obtained almost exclusively from sheep, with Australia producing 30 per cent of the world's wool requirements. Other animals such as Kashmir goats are reared for their wool, known as cashmere, but this is a small selective area of woollen production.

Wool is twisted and spun into a continuous strand from the short fibres of the sheep. These woollen strands are then mixed to form smooth or textured, thick or fine yarn for knitting or weaving into a variety of fabrics. Wool fabric is warm, flexible and able to absorb water easily for dyeing. However, it is sensitive to high temperatures and careful washing and handling is needed when dyeing and decorating. It can be dyed deep, vibrant shades of colours and is used for a variety of purposes ranging from strong woollen fabric for upholstery to fine woollen suiting.

- **Dyes** Acid dyes, natural dyes.
- **Techniques** Screenprinting (page 50), block printing (page 48).
- **Wool recipes** Indigo (page 72), chamomile yellow (page 104), walnut twist (page 75) and two-colour magic (page 78).

Nylon

Nylon is a synthetic man-made fabric now known as polyamide. Developed in 1935 by the American chemist Wallace H. Carothers, it became best known for stockings in the 1940s and 1950s. It is still used extensively in the manufacture of hosiery and lingerie due to its ability to stretch when cold and mould well to the body. It is also used for numerous commercial products such as tents, mesh sieves and toothbrushes. Stretch nylon, or lycra, is often combined with cotton to produce T-shirts, with the better quality garments having up to 30% nylon lycra content. Nylon is frequently used to make waterproof garments as it is easy to cover with a protective coating. This, of course, needs removing before any dyeing or decorating techniques take place. Nylon can be dyed and decorated quite easily at home using acid dye powder colours or any of the surface pigment colours and effects.

- **Dyes** Acid dyes, hot- or cold-water dyes.
- **Techniques** Screenprinting (page 50), stencilling (page 46).
- **Nylon recipes** Acid on nylon (page 122), textured effect (page 133).

Viscose

A man-made fabric, viscose can be dyed and decorated with the same dyes that work well with natural cellulose fabrics, such as cotton. Unlike cotton, however, viscose does not absorb natural dyes well.

Viscose was first produced in 1892 and is manufactured by breaking down wood pulp with a strong alkaline solution. Though usually recognized by its shiny finish, it can be both matt and shiny in appearance and is available in a wide range of fabric weights. It absorbs dyeing and decorating powders and pastes well and easily produces intense colours evenly across the whole of the fabric. It is often combined with cotton to produce a fabric with some of cotton's natural characteristics, but at a lower cost. It is a hard-wearing and durable fabric used for both fashion and interior textiles.

- **Dyes** Hot- or cold-water dyes, reactive dyes.
- **Techniques** Stencilling (page 46), block printing (page 48), monoprinting (page 52)
- **Viscose recipes** Glitter painting (page 136), foil dot (page 116), colour direct (page 95).

Polyester

Polyester is a man-made, synthetic fabric that was first developed in Britain by ICI in 1941. It is the strongest fabric and so is used in a wide range of manufacturing industries, including textiles (silkscreen mesh is made of mono-filament polyester). It is able to withstand high temperatures and frequent washing, and the strong,

continuous fibres can now even be made from recycled plastics. It can be heat-set into various shapes and forms such as pleats. Polyester fibre is also available in a transparent form, making an extremely light and sheer fabric.

Polyester is often combined with other fibres such as linen, cotton and wool to make hard-wearing mixed-fibre fabrics useful for the craft dyer. Polyester needs to be dyed at high temperatures with chemical assistants and when decorating, it must be processed at high temperatures or with steam, under pressure.

- **Dyes** Disperse dyes.
- **Techniques** Screenprinting (page 50), wax printing (page 54), stencilling (page 46).
- **Polyester recipes** Transfer squares (page 142), wire and polyester (page 143), polyester painting (page 126).

Mixed fibres

A wide variety of textiles available today are made up of a mixture of fibres. Some of the techniques and recipes in this book, such as devoré and cross-dyeing, rely on this mix of fibres in the fabric for the chemical reactions to take place.

The recent developments in textiles containing a mix of natural and synthetic fibres has greatly expanded the possibilities for dyeing and decorating fabric such as velvet. Previously, velvet was made either of 100 per cent silk, which was very expensive, or 100 per cent cotton for the mass market. Today, however, strong velvet ideal for upholstery is available with a synthetic backing and silk pile. Velvet used in the fashion industry has a silk backing and viscose pile and is particularly suitable for devoré techniques.

- **Dyes** Dependent on the fabric – may need two recipes at one time.
- **Techniques** Devoré (page 56), dying mixed yarns (page 62).
- **Recipes** Cross-dyed velvet (page 100).

Identifying yarns

Identifying the fibres that go together to make up a yarn can help you to decide which of the recipes you will be able to follow successfully.

To identify yarn you can use the same burn test as described for fabric on pages 18–19. A small twist of thread or wrapping of yarn is all that is needed to check what is the fibre content of your yarn. However, most yarn is labelled with its content, as it is sold in a different way to fabric, which is generally cut off a reel in the shop, and is identified by its design rather than its fibre content. Like fabric, yarn can be categorized according to whether it is made from natural, synthetic or mixed fibres. Yarns also come in a huge range of thicknesses, counts or deniers, qualities and strengths which in turn have a wide variety of uses.

Modern yarns are often coated with different types of chemicals and finishes that enable manufacturers to make up garments that, for example, allow perspiration to pass through the garment, or prevent irritation, giving relief to eczema sufferers.

Dyeing your own yarns gives you the opportunity to knit, weave, crochet or embroider with the exact fibre you want in your own customized colours and shades, unrestricted by what is available in the shops. If you weave or knit, there are endless combinations of patterns and effects that can be created by mixing yarns and colours. The variety provided by the recipes in this book will bring a new creative dimension to your work.

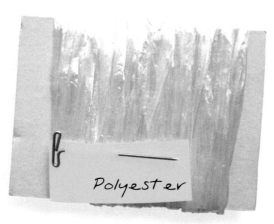

Cotton

Cellulose yarn or cotton comes from the cotton plant, *Gossypium*. It can range from fine cotton threads for sewing, to thick heavy ropes for ships. It is a strong, easy-to-use yarn that dyes with both natural and synthetic dyes.

Linen

The oldest yarn, it is more commonly woven into fabric than knitted. It is extremely strong and hard-wearing, and items made from linen age well. Dyes with both natural and synthetic dyes.

Silk

Silk yarn can be made up into the most luxurious of fabrics. When coloured with either natural or synthetic dyes, which silk absorbs readily and easily, it produces the most glorious intensely coloured fabrics and yarns available.

Wool

Woollen yarn is available in a wide range of thicknesses and textures, ranging from fine weights for baby clothes, to heavy knits for fishermen's sweaters. It can be dyed with almost the entire range of natural dyes, as well as with synthetic acid dyes.

Nylon

Nylon or polyamide is an amazing synthetic yarn with an ability to stretch without heat, making it ideal for underwear and hoisery production. It can produce the most startling of fluorescent results when coloured with synthetic acid dyes.

Viscose

Viscose yarn is often mixed with other fibres to produce a wide range of fabrics for both fashion and interiors. It is made from broken down wood pulp, and dyes well with both direct and reactive synthetic dyes.

Polyester

As polyester is a manufactured yarn it can be spun to match any requirements. Other yarns, including natural ones, are often coated in polyester to combine the qualities of both yarns. It needs to be dyed at a high temperature with disperse dye.

Mixed fibres

You can buy yarn made from a combination of fibres, or you can combine yarns yourself. Each yarn needs to be dyed with the appropriate dye, but often this can be done in one container. Some interesting effects can be achieved by mixing fibres.

Preparing fabrics and yarns

Before you start any of the recipes in this book, you will need to prepare your fabric or yarn carefully to ensure successful results. First it is important to identify your fabric so that you choose an appropriate dye and recipe. You will also need to weigh your fabric to establish the amount of dyes or chemicals you will need. Your fabric or yarn may also require washing to remove any finishes, such as starch, wax or gum, so that the fabric will pick up the dye evenly across the whole of the piece.

Washing Wetting the fabric thoroughly and washing off any finishes before you start a recipe enables the dye to penetrate evenly and easily.

Washing

Fabric can be washed in a washing machine following the manufacturer's instructions for the fabric type. However, it is more common to wash fabrics and yarn by hand when preparing them for dyeing. Although some fabrics may only need a short handwash, other fabrics such as silk may require a long hot wash to remove all the residue finishes. When handwashing, use a small amount of mild detergent – a handwash powder or liquid with a neutral pH is ideal.

Testing your fabric

It is important to know exactly what kind of fibres make up a piece of fabric because different fibres require different dyes. Using the wrong dye for your fibre type can result in failure and disappointment. If you are unsure about the make-up of fibres in any fabric you want to use, you can use a very simple burn test to find out the fibre content. All you need to do is cut a small sample of your fabric and then carefully set it alight in controlled conditions. Observe the sample carefully, because each fibre type will burn in a specific way, producing different coloured smoke, a particular smell and leaving its own kind of residue. To match your findings with the correct fibre, consult the illustration and chart opposite.

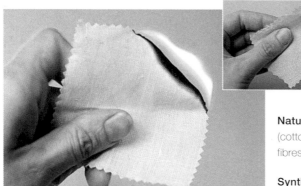

Natural fibres (left) Grouped into cellulose fibres (cotton, linen) and protein fibres (wool, silk), natural fibres burn with a bright flame when set alight.

Synthetic fibres (inset) Nylon and polyester, both synthetic fibres, melt and do not burn brightly when set alight.

The burn test

The chart at the bottom of the page will enable you to identify your fabric or yarn fibre by the simple burn test given on page 18. Shown below are the eight main fibre groups after applying this test. Mixed fibres will always produce conflicting results, and so are not shown in the table. Always try to find out their composition before buying. If you can't ascertain this, then it will be a matter of using trial and error to work out which recipes are most suitable.

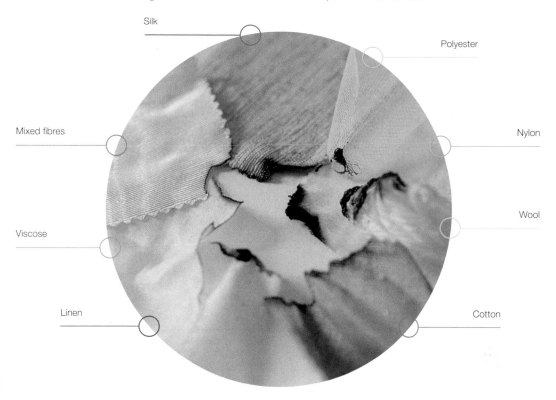

	Burns or melts	Flame	Smoke colour	Speed	Smell	Crumble factor
Cotton	Burns	Yellow	Grey	Fast	Burning paper	Soft, grey feathery fine ash
Linen	Burns	Yellow	Grey	Fast	Burning paper	Soft, grey feathery fine ash
Silk	Burns	Irregular	Grey	Slow	Burning hair or feathers	Easily crushable ash, brittle
Wool	Burns	Irregular	Grey	Slow	Burning hair or feathers	Easily crushable ash, brittle
Nylon	Melts	Yellow	Grey	Quite fast	Cooked celery	Hard uncrushable brown bead
Viscose	Burns	Yellow	Grey	Fast	Burning paper	Soft, grey feathery fine ash
Polyester	Melts	Yellow	Grey	Quite fast	Aromatic, sweetish hot oil	Hard uncrushable brown bead

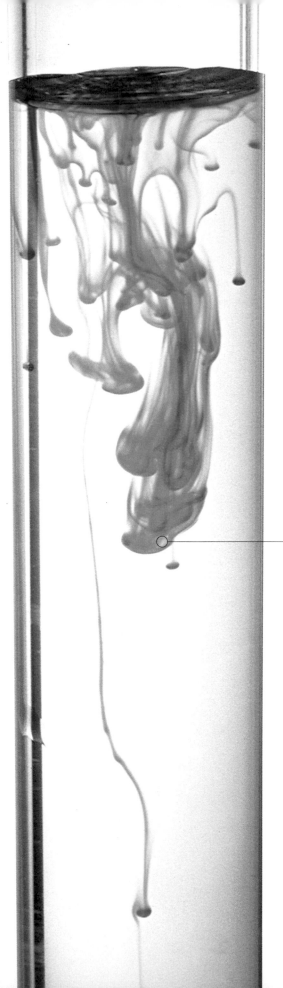

All about dyes

The wide range of fabric dyes available – both natural and synthetic – may at first sight seem bewildering. However, a knowledge of the characteristics and usage of each dye type will help you to select a suitable dye for creating your colour scheme on your chosen fabric.

Synthetic dyes

The advantage of using synthetic dyes is their light- and wash-fastness, which far exceeds those of natural dyestuffs. The first synthetic dye – a lavender colour – was produced from coal tar by William Henry Perkins in the late 1850s. Today's synthetic dyes can be used safely to colour many different types of fabric and yarn types and are available in a wide range of vibrant colours.

Most synthetic dyes look dull in powder form (see facing page) and only reveal their brilliance when added to a medium, such as water. For this reason always do a test sample on the fabric or yarn first before embarking on a large dyeing project.

White pigment colour

Glitter powder

Pearlized pigment colour

Direct dye

Acid dye

Disperse dye

Reactive dye

A good method of testing the colour shade of a dye powder is to dissolve a few grains in water first.

Synthetic dyes come mainly in powder or paste form and are widely available from craft outlets as well as specialist suppliers. There are several types of synthetic dye powder, each of which is formulated for use on specific fabrics or for a specific application.

Acid dyes Fabulous vibrant colours can be achieved with acid dyes. They are suitable for dyeing protein fibres such as wool and silk, and also nylon if a higher temperature is used. They can be used in hot-water vat dyeing or be painted or printed in paste form. See recipes on pages 89, 102, 119, 120 and 146.

Direct dyes Also known as substantive dyes, direct dyes are suitable for vat dyeing and painting cellulose fibres such as cotton and linen. They can also be used to dye viscose. See recipes on pages 95,

Pure pigment colour for use on all fabric types

100 and 118.

Disperse dyes Brilliant light-fast colours on polyester are produced with disperse dyes. They can be vat dyed, painted and printed. See recipes on pages 83, 126 and 142.

Reactive dyes Clear and light-fast colours can be achieved with reactive dyes. They are available for cold- or hot-water vat dyeing and painting on cotton, linen and silk. See recipes on pages 79, 90, 113 and 117.

Pigment Dyes Pigment dye colours can be used on almost any fabric, for painting or printing. There is a wide range of binders available to use with the colours enabling you to create different effects as your fabric varies. See pages 112, 123, 133 and 135.

Natural dyes

Evidence of madder on cotton string found in India suggests that natural dyeing took place as long ago as 3000BC. A thousand years later, in 2000BC, the Egyptians added mordants to natural dyes to make their fabrics colourfast. Over the years natural dyes have been put to numerous and varied uses by civilizations throughout the world. Many of these natural dyes used since ancient times are still produced and in use today, although some, such as indigo, have now mainly been replaced by synthetic equivalents. For the home dyer and decorator, the main attraction of natural dyes is the beauty and subtlety of colour that they can produce. Natural dyes can also be combined to produce a wide range of colours and shades.

An added advantage of using natural dyes is that they can be produced simply at home. Many are made from common plants that can be easily cultivated in the garden, such as onions and apples More exotic is fustic, dyestuff obtained from wood chips from the tree, *Chlorophora tinctoria*. Remember also that many plants yield more than

Blackberries

Fustic

Acorns

Cochineal

Logwood

one colour. For example, you can get two colours from the blackberry: lilac from the berry and shades of green-grey from the leaves and shoots. Whilst you can, with practice, produce a similar beauty and subtlety with synthetic dye powders, there is something special about a piece of fabric that you dyed from a plant you grew yourself in your garden.

Some natural dyes are not made from plants: Tyrian purple was obtained from a species of shellfish. However, since it required up to 20,000 of them to produce 1g of dye, it is not used any more! Cochineal, obtained from the body of the female cochineal louse, has been used as a natural red dye for thousands of years. Although it takes thousands of insects to make a small amount of dye, it produces a strong, permanent colour.

Ivy leaves

Weld

Dyer's alkanet

Pickable natural dyes and their colours

oak bark and leaves	*plum and green*
apple bark and leaves	*brown and green*
onion skins	*yellow and brown*
blackberry fruit, leaves and shoots	*lilac and grey*
ivy leaves and shoots	*green*
blackthorn fruit and shoots	*lilac and green*
walnut leaves	*brown and green*
dandelion flowers and leaves	*yellow and green*
pear bark and leaves	*plum and green*
rhubarb shoots	*orange and green*

There are also some natural dyes not obtained from plants, eg Tyrian purple, cochineal.

Apple bark and fruit

Turmeric

Mordanting and fixing

The natural dyes featured in this book work best on natural fibres. Almost all fabrics for natural dyeing need to be chemically treated first to make the dyes fix and remain fast on the fibres. This process, known as mordanting, needs to be carried out carefully, following the instructions below.

The process

First weigh your fabric to establish how much mordant and dye you will need and then wash it to remove any surface finishes. The mordant ingredients are mixed together and added to the dye container with the fabric. The fabric is

---

Mordant mix for wool and silk weighing 100g (4oz)

- 7g (½tblsp) alum
- 7g (½tblsp) cream of tartar
- 150ml (⅔ cup) warm water

You can also use aluminium ammonium sulphate. You will need to increase the amount slightly because it is not as strong.

Mordant mix for cotton and linen weighing 100g (4oz)

- 50g (4tsp) alum
- 50g (4tsp) tannic acid
- 200ml (1cup) warm water

Follow the instructions below to mordant cotton and linen; after simmering for 1 hour, leave the fabric to stand in the mixture overnight.

Mordanting fabric

1 Wash the fabric in a mild detergent and rinse in cold water. Wearing safety clothing, mix all the ingredients together in a glass or metal dye-mixing pot.

2 Fill a metal dye container with enough cold water to cover the fabric. Add the fabric and the mordant mixed in step 1.

3 Slowly bring the dye container to the boil and then allow to simmer for approximately 1 hour.

4 Remove the fabric with tongs and rinse in cold water. The fabric can now be dyed with natural dyes.

brought to the boil and simmered for an hour in this mixture. After rinsing in cold water, the fabric is ready to be dyed with natural dyes.

Mordanting for natural dyes

Throughout this book, the mordant for silk and wool is a mixture of potassium aluminium sulphate, commonly known as alum, and potassium hydrogen tartrate, or cream of tartar. Although alum can be used on its own, it is an environmentally unfriendly chemical. By adding the cream of tartar, you can ensure that almost all of the alum goes onto the fibre and very little, if any, is washed away into the environment.

After-mordants

Many natural dyes can have their natural colour altered – either dulled or enhanced – by the addition of an after-mordant. This can either be applied to the fabric or yarn at the same time as the dye liquid itself or afterwards in a separate container. Some of the chemicals used as after-mordants are extremely dangerous and extra care needs to be taken when handling and storing them.

Iron ferric sulphate, one of the oldest mordants, is used mainly to dull or "sadden" a colour. Stannous chloride is used to enhance or brighten colours. Note that it is a poison and irritant, so extra care must be taken at all times when handling and storing.

Steaming Some dyes need to be fixed by pressure steaming. Wrap the fabric in calico and foil and place on a tray above the water in a pressure steamer.

Fixing the dye

The dyes used in the recipes in this book are fixed by a variety of methods, including heat, simmering, steaming and oxidation. A hot iron applied to the back of the fabric, or a hair dryer on the front, will fix many of the dyes used in the Painting and Printing sections of the book (pages 111–154). Always take care to check the iron setting is not too high, particularly when ironing synthetic fabrics.

High-temperature simmering is the most common method used to fix dyes in the vat-dyeing section of the book (see pages 69–109). Most of the recipes here require the fabric to be brought to the boil and then simmered for a period. Always take care when heating dye containers – always wear gloves and safety clothing and use tongs to handle hot fabric. Never overheat fabrics, because this can affect the fabric's basic qualities, ruining silk and felting wool, for example.

Some recipes in this book require the dye to be fixed by steaming. This can be done in a wok or in a pressure cooker. If the recipe requires pressure steaming, use only the pressure cooker. Note that this equipment, once used for fabric decorating, must never be used for food preparation.

Some dyes, notably indigo (see page 72), are fixed by leaving them to oxidize in the open air.

> **Dulling after-mordant for 100g (4oz) dry weight fabric or yarn**
>
> • 5g (1tsp) iron ferric sulphate
> Wearing safety clothing, add iron ferric sulphate to the dye container, about 30 minutes before removing the fabric or yarn from the container.
>
> **Brightening after-mordant for 100g (4oz) dry weight fabric or yarn**
>
> • 4g (¾tsp) stannous chloride
> Wearing safety clothing, add stannous chloride to the dye container about 30 minutes before removing the fabric or yarn from the container.

Basic equipment and materials

Before you start to dye or decorate, it is essential to set aside a work area that is clean and well-lit, ideally with natural light for colour matching and testing and with enough space to work easily. Always check the equipment list in each recipe so that you have all the items you will need to hand, such as brushes for painting, string or rubber bands for resists and blocks and stencils for patterning. Note that many recipes, particularly those using pastes, require you to press the fabric well with a hot iron before you start.

Dye containers

If your chosen recipe involves vat dyeing, you will need a stainless steel pan. Large cooking

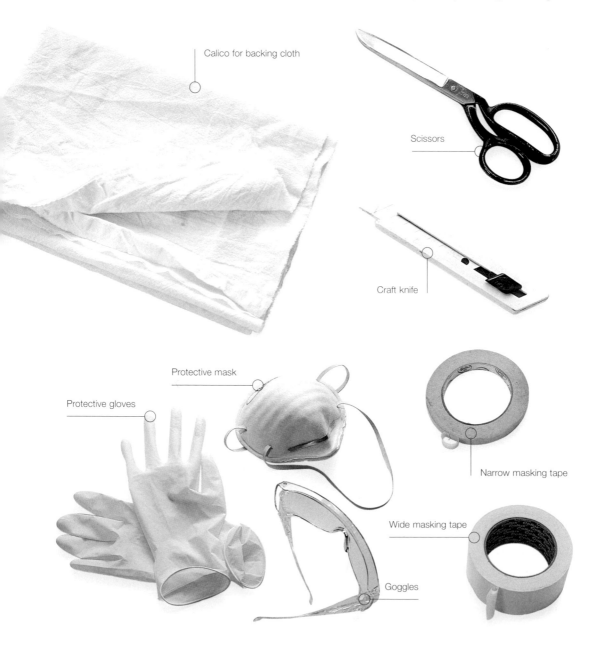

Calico for backing cloth

Scissors

Craft knife

Protective mask

Protective gloves

Narrow masking tape

Wide masking tape

Goggles

Large brush

Tongs

Small brush

Medium brush

Sponge

Dropper

Sponge

Plain newsprint

Dye container

pots, such as those intended for commercial catering, are particularly suitable because they can hold the volume of water needed to colour fabrics successfully. For most of the container dyeing recipes you will need to be able to heat this container. A small, separate electric or gas hob is best for this purpose, so that you can site your work area away from the kitchen and food. If you have no choice but to use your kitchen cooker, make sure that all food and cooking equipment is stored safely away from the dyeing area.

When following a vat-dyeing recipe, you will need to take extra care in handling the large containers of boiling water. Always check that you are able to lift and handle them yourself and make sure no person or child can knock them over. If in doubt at any time during the vat-dyeing process, carefully remove the fabric from the container and leave the liquid to cool before handling.

Dye pots for mixing

You will also need a selection of glass, plastic or metal mixing pots for mixing dyes, chemicals and pastes. Note that these must be used for this purpose only. If you use food containers it is very important that you remove labels to avoid confusion. Always label dye containers with the contents and the date mixed so that they are readily identifiable. You will need a selection of different sized containers for the various ingredients mixed in the recipes

Weighing equipment

For weighing out dye powders and chemicals, it is best to use the most accurate scales you can find. They need to be able to weigh very small amounts so that you can measure out the dye

Metal mixing jug

Plastic mixing pot

Weighing scales

Measuring spoons

Measuring pots

Glass mixing pots

Metal spatula

Stirring spoon

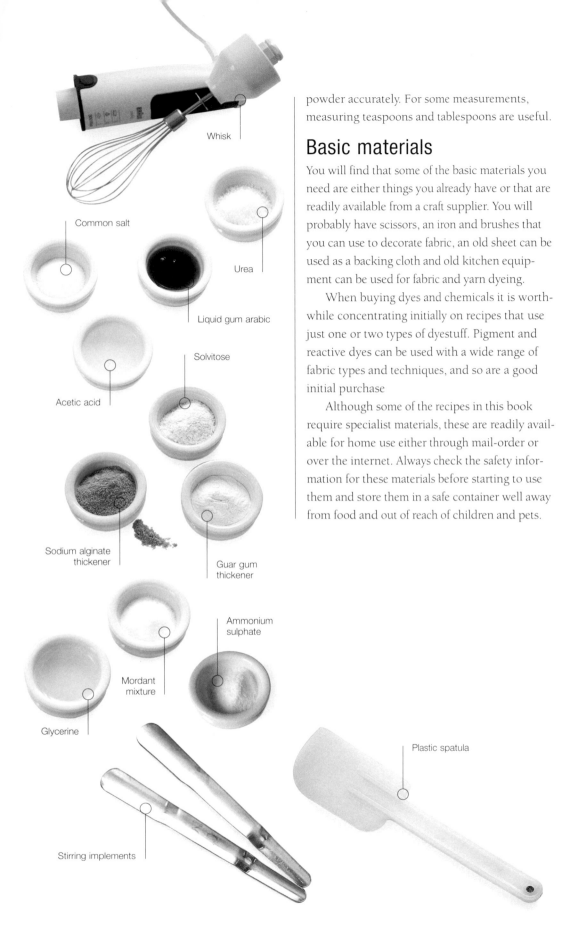

Whisk

Common salt

Urea

Liquid gum arabic

Solvitose

Acetic acid

Sodium alginate
thickener

Guar gum
thickener

Ammonium
sulphate

Mordant
mixture

Glycerine

Plastic spatula

Stirring implements

powder accurately. For some measurements, measuring teaspoons and tablespoons are useful.

Basic materials

You will find that some of the basic materials you need are either things you already have or that are readily available from a craft supplier. You will probably have scissors, an iron and brushes that you can use to decorate fabric, an old sheet can be used as a backing cloth and old kitchen equipment can be used for fabric and yarn dyeing.

When buying dyes and chemicals it is worthwhile concentrating initially on recipes that use just one or two types of dyestuff. Pigment and reactive dyes can be used with a wide range of fabric types and techniques, and so are a good initial purchase

Although some of the recipes in this book require specialist materials, these are readily available for home use either through mail-order or over the internet. Always check the safety information for these materials before starting to use them and store them in a safe container well away from food and out of reach of children and pets.

Planning your work area

The area you choose as your work space must be well-lit and easy to clean, with your tools and materials readily to hand. Plan it in much the same manner as a kitchen, so that you can dye and decorate fabrics and yarns without constantly moving from space to space.

As some of the recipes and techniques featured in this book involve leaving processes to take effect for a period of time, for example indigo dyeing, you will need a work area that will allow you to leave pots, fabric and tools out overnight, safely away from children and pets. As your interest in dyeing and decorating your own fabrics grows, you may want to buy additional equipment and materials and these will also need to be stored somewhere. You will need to ensure

Making a simple work board

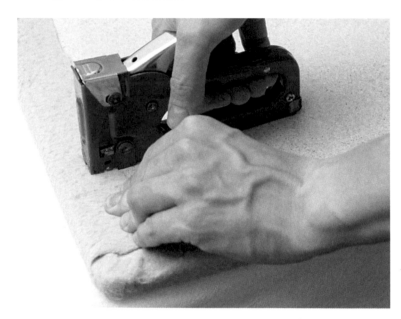

1 Choose a piece of 1.2cm (½in) chipboard, blockboard or MDF (medium density fibreboard) slightly larger than the fabric you will be decorating, and cover it with a blanket. This needs to be firmly stretched over the board and secured with a staple gun on the underside, leaving the work surface smooth and wrinkle-free. Stapling alternate sides of the board, work from the middle of the sides towards the corners, folding them over neatly to finish.

2 Now cover with thick plastic sheet or PVC and stretch it firmly and smoothly over the surface. Attach to the board with a staple gun.

3 Work from the middle of the board outwards to ensure a flat smooth work surface.

that you can reach all the fabric you are painting or printing, and that your work surface is at a comfortable height so that you can work without straining. Your work area will also need to be warm and well-ventilated.

Decorating surface

If your chosen recipe involves painting or printing a design onto fabric, you will need a suitable work surface on which you can pin and tape fabric flat. A flat work board which you can place on a table or any firm surface is ideal. The board should also be easy to clean so that it can be re-used. If you plan to do a lot of fabric painting and decorating, you can make a more durable work surface by covering a table with a plastic or PVC covering. First, cover the table with a thick blanket, pull it taut and staple it to the table. Cover this with plastic or PVC sheeting and again, pull it taut and staple it on the under-side as shown left. Then cover this with a back-ing cloth of calico, or an old clean sheet, glued in place with a thin layer of liquid gum arabic (see right). This backing cloth can be easily removed for washing between decorating sessions.

Dye container area

If you are dyeing your fabric following most of the recipes in this book, you will need either to use your kitchen cooker, or invest in a separate gas or electric ring to heat the fabrics and dyes.

To use your kitchen cooker safely, certain precautions must be followed. Do not cook or prepare food at the same time as you are work-ing with dye; cover all food preparation areas with paper or plastic while dyeing and NEVER cook or prepare food using pans and other containers or utensils that have been used for dyeing.

Ideally, it is best to have a totally separate portable heating ring for fabric and yarn dyeing. This can be gas or electricity operated, but you must ensure that the ring is big enough to comfortably hold large dye containers without any risk of them toppling over.

Making a table cover

1 Lightly gum a thick plastic or PVC surface with a thin layer of liquid gum arabic using a squeegee, old credit card or spatula. Allow to dry.

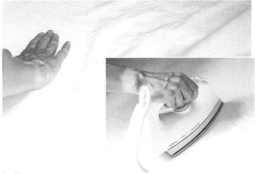

2 Place a sheet of calico, cheap plain white cotton, as a backing cloth over the surface and steam press onto the surface using a steam iron. Make sure there are no wrinkles because these can affect the fabric to be decorated.

3 Now pin your fabric to this cloth, making sure that the pins are flat against the surface (especially if you are screenprinting) and do not damage the plastic surface. Alternatively you can lightly iron your fabric directly onto the gum arabic – the gum arabic will wash off and not affect your work.

Choosing your design

Think back to the last time you bought something made of fabric. It is safe to say that it was either the colour, texture or pattern that first attracted you to the piece. Even some of the most minimalist looking fabrics do have a subtle pattern or design, even though this may not be immediately obvious. One of the hardest tasks faced by the fabric decorator is deciding exactly how to pattern a piece of fabric.

Finding inspiration

One of the easiest methods of choosing a design is to collect pictures, colours and patterns that you like and then stick them in a scrapbook to make a source book of inspirational ideas. These could be holiday photographs of the sea, the colours in a market place, or the colours of the landscape. Try putting together magazine pictures of fabrics, ceramics or glass with amazing textures, patterns and colours. If you find paint charts, seashells or driftwood with colours and patterns that you like, save them for future reference. Look around your house – you may find that you already have a collection of colourful items such as cups, glasses or beads that you can use as a starting point to decorate your own fabrics.

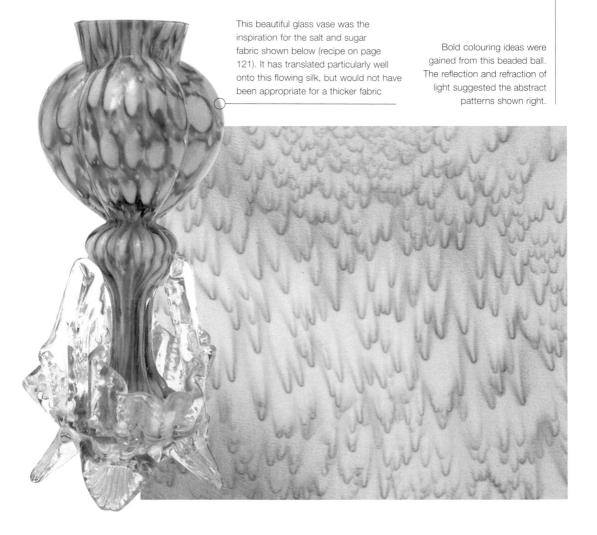

This beautiful glass vase was the inspiration for the salt and sugar fabric shown below (recipe on page 121). It has translated particularly well onto this flowing silk, but would not have been appropriate for a thicker fabric

Bold colouring ideas were gained from this beaded ball. The reflection and refraction of light suggested the abstract patterns shown right.

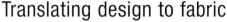

Variations These abstract patterns have been developed in several scales and with varying amounts of colour. One idea can often be developed in this way to produce several designs, which can be used on fabrics for a variety of purpose.

Translating design to fabric

Look at the pictures or objects you have collected and try to analyze what it is that you like about the separate elements within your items. Is it the colour or the proportions of colour? Is it the pattern or design that attracts you? Try to think how this will translate onto the fabric you want to decorate. Do you need all the colours or will just the main colour or coloured elements be enough for your fabric? Do you need to use all of the images from the picture or object or just one, or even just a part of one?

Think carefully about how you may want to use the finished piece of fabric, as this will also have a strong bearing on your design. If you like mainly pale, neutral clothing and interiors, you may want to decorate fabrics to continue this theme. If you like bold, strong colour and pattern, you will perhaps want to expand this colour scheme. You may want to decorate fabrics to give as gifts or even to sell, in which case you need to consider the recipient of the gift, but still retain your own sense of design and colour so that the recipient knows that you have decorated the fabric.

Using scale in your design

You may want to make a big, bold statement, in which case you could have just one extremely large image on your fabric. Alternatively, you may decide to use a small image and repeat this over the fabric. The scale you choose will be influenced by the final use of your fabric. An oversized image will not work so well on a scarf but brilliantly as a wall hanging whereas the smaller scale image will work better on a smaller piece.

You can use the same initial source material in different scales. You can scale up the outline shape of flowers, for example, to create an overall background pattern and then overprint these with the smaller scale colours and details of flowers.

Proportion of a design

You can either keep to the same proportions as the pattern and colours from your inspirational image or change them to fit in with the end use of your fabric. It can sometimes help to measure the proportions and write them down, so that you can then translate them to your fabric in a more abstracted form by either changing the proportions or colours or even adding in other design elements. In a similar way, you can change the position of your design image when you put it on a piece of fabric. Although the design may be in the middle of your inspirational image, you could try, for example, moving it to the edge of your fabric and seeing how it looks there.

Using colour

We are surrounded by colour all the time in our everyday lives and even when we try to block this out by dressing in black or living in a white space we are still surrounded by colour; the food we eat, the plants and flowers we walk by, the landscape we live in can all influence and direct our use of colour.

Some of the recipes in this book, particularly those using natural dyes, will dictate the colour that you will dye or pattern your fabric. However, in many of the recipes, you will need to choose the colour yourself. It can be very daunting to be faced with a blank piece of fabric to decorate, pattern and colour, but with careful thought and planning a successful outcome can be achieved. When you have planned a colour scheme, always test dye or decorate several small sample pieces of fabric, within the same fabric type, to check which will be most successful for

The colour wheel can help you to decide which colours will complement or contrast with each other.

your finished piece. Always keep a small piece of any fabric or yarn that you dye in a notebook with details of the dye used, how much and for how long, even if you decide not to use that colour at the time. This notebook will build up over time to be your own personal reference of colours and how to achieve them and will be an invaluable source for future dye projects.

Colour inspiration

You can use your design inspiration scrapbook to give you colour ideas – you will find that the strengths and proportions of colur in nature: flowers, animals, birds, insects and sea life all work well together and your work can reflect this. If in doubt about which colour to use, ask a child his or her favourite colour and go with that!

Alternatively you could colour your fabrics to fit in with their intended use. For example, you might choose a simple, light wash of colour over silk to be made into a shirt to wear with a formal suit. You could use a bold, striking colour on

Below Fabric swatches **a** and **b** show the same fabric, dyed by the same method, but swatch **b** was left in the vat for longer. Swatches **c** and **d** are different fabrics that were dyed for the same length of time in the same dye.

a **b** **c** **d**

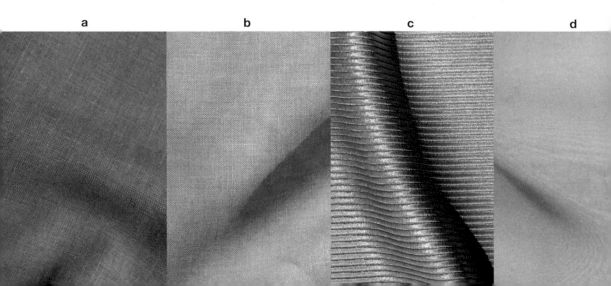

dye yarn in blue and orange, to knit into a garment with contrasting stripes

By varying the intensity of a colour, you can give yourself a whole range of shades to work with, as shown in the recipe for one-colour shading on page 102. The only point to remember is that it can often be the level of intensity or depth of shade of a colour that does not work well with another colour, not the colour itself.

Colours will also look very different on different fabrics. It is worthwhile experimenting with dyeing and patterning a variety of fabrics with a particular shade or method before making a final decision. Transparent, opaque, matt and shiny fabrics can all give very different results.

fabric for an armchair cushion to liven up an area, or the colour can simply fit in with the rest of your house or wardrobe's colour scheme.

Understanding colours

By using a simple colour wheel you can work out which colours work harmoniously together and which can be used to create a more vivid colour scheme. Colours next to each other on the colour wheel will go well with each other – for example, red with oranges and yellows and reds with purples and blues. If you want a contrasting colour, look at the opposite side of the colour wheel – for example, you could dye a fabric purple and then add a golden-yellow design. Similarly, you could

Below Fabric swatches **e** and **f** show the same fabric dyed with different strengths of dye for the same length of time. Swatches **g** and **h** show the different effects of dyeing on shiny, **g**, and matt, **h**, fabrics.

e	f	g	h

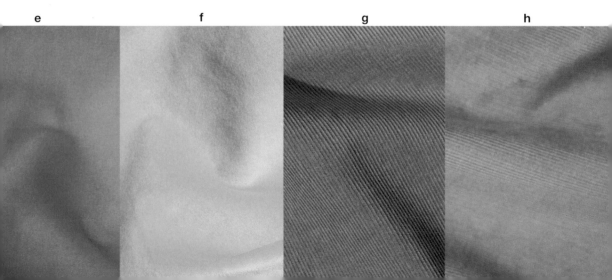

Repeat patterns

One of the most commonly used design elements in decorated fabrics is the repeat. Fabric with repeat designs and patterns has been found that dates from thousands of years ago. Today these ancient pattern formations are still used to repeat a pattern or motif onto fabric.

Even on relatively small pieces of fabric, you can make a pattern with a repeated motif. This can range from a simple bottle cork pattern, as in the recipe for spreading print on page 146 to a more complex intercutting design where it is not so easy to see the individual design elements, as in the leafy print recipe on page 140.

Registration techniques

To achieve a successful repeat pattern you need to mark your fabric with accurate register points. Using a soft pencil, erasable textile pen or tailor's chalk you can lightly mark the fabric with a grid or plan of the repeat motif.

If you are using a silkscreen, you can use masking tape to mark the outside edges of the screen on your printing table, so that you will know where on the fabric the screen will go each time. Masking tape is also useful for guiding you in other registration requirements. You can also try taping fine threads across the fabric to guide you in your design repeat.

With block printing it is usual to have pins at the edges of the block, which are also printed and give a guide as to where the next block should be placed.

Practice will determine which method suits your needs best, and you may find that a mixture of registration techniques gives the best results.

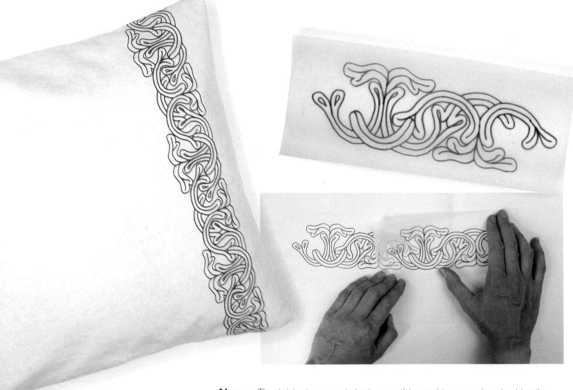

Above The intricate repeat design on this cushion was inspired by the border in gold thread shown on page 37. First one section of the design was isolated and then photocopied to create the repeat pattern.

a

b

c

Designing with repeats

There are many repeat patterns, such as the full-drop repeat and triangle repeat, that you can use to design or structure your image on fabric. You may decide to cover all your fabric or you may decide to use a repeat design just to decorate the border of your fabric. Repeats of lines, circles, crosses, spirals, zigzags, dots and chevrons were particularly popular in the Roman and Egyptian periods for decorating the edges of clothing. The repeat patterns shown here are of a geometric nature, but you can add to the design by placing additional images within the structure.

Above and below One isolated design element (see below) can produce several different effects. A half-drop repeat, **a**, forms an interesting line design, while turning the pattern on end, **b**, and also left and right, **c**, and repeating creates an intricate geometric design.

techniques

The techniques shown here describe the basic methods of decorating fabric and yarn featured in the recipes. Once you have mastered the techniques, you will be able to intermix and expand the design and colour possibilities to create your own wonderful fabrics. Use this section as a reference and to experiment, but do keep notes so you can re-create the effect!

Vat dyeing

Vat dyeing, or container dyeing, is one of the simplest ways to colour and pattern a piece of fabric. In the technique, the fabric is immersed in a metal container with the dye and plenty of water to ensure even distribution of the dye colour. You can pattern fabric at the same time by using tie-dye techniques (see page 42).

Both natural dyes and synthetic dyes can be used in the vat. Natural dyes produce an amazing quality of colour, from the jewel-like brightness of chamomile yellow (see page 104) to the subtlety of oak bark and acorns (see page 81). The wide range of synthetic dyes available enables you to dye almost any fabric any colour.

All the vat recipes in this book indicate the amount of dye to be used based on the dry fabric or yarn weighing 100g (4oz) before dyeing unless stated otherwise. For a heavier weight of fabric, increase the amount of dye and fixative and decrease for a light-weight fabric. For a stronger colour, gradually increase the dye by about 0.5g (⅛tsp) per 100g (4oz) of fabric. Decrease the amount of dye by the same quantity for a lighter colour. Practise first and keep a record of your dye tests.

Equipment
Safety clothing
Metal dye container
Glass or metal dye pots
  for mixing
Tongs
Spatula

Basic recipe for approx. 1sq m (9sq ft) thick cotton weighing 250g (10oz)
2.5g (½tsp) light
  red direct dye powder
  dissolved in 100ml
  (½ cup) hot water
25g (1oz) household salt

1 After washing the fabric, fill a metal dye container with plenty of cold water. Add the fabric to the container and pour in the dissolved dye colour. Take care not to pour the dye directly onto the fabric.

2 Slowly raise the temperature of the contents of the container to 80°C (176°F), or just below boiling point. Allow to simmer for 30 to 60 minutes, stirring frequently to ensure even distribution of the dye.

3 While the temperature is rising, you will need to add the salt. Wearing safety clothing and using tongs, first remove the fabric to prevent the salt going directly onto the fabric. Add the salt – you can either add it all at once or in two stages 5 to 10 minutes apart to allow the fabric a chance to pick up the salt over a period of time. Replace the fabric and allow it to continue dyeing.

4 To check how the fabric is taking up the dye, wear safety clothing and remove the container from the heat. Squeeze out excess water and dye from a corner of the fabric to see how dyeing is progressing.

5 When the fabric has reached the required colour, remove from the container and rinse in plenty of cold running water and leave to dry. Remember to wash your equipment after use ready for the next time.

Tie-dyeing

Tie-dyeing is one of the oldest methods of creating a pattern by using a physical resist to prevent dye reaching the bound areas of the fabric. In the technique, the resist is formed by tying the fabric into shapes and patterns with strong thread or rubber bands. You can also try tying objects such as fruit seeds, marbles, gravel or even keys into your fabric to add an extra element of design. After dyeing, the fabric is untied to reveal patterns created by the ties. Related methods include folding, pleating, twisting, clamping and shibori, an ancient Japanese technique in which running stitches on fabric are pulled tightly to form the resist.

The possibilities for patterning are endless: you can tie the fabric following a strict repeat design pattern, or for a more random effect try placing the ties or objects freely across the fabric. Once you have tied your fabric, dye using the vat-dyeing technique (see page 40). Many recipes in the vat-dyeing section of this book show you how to create fabulous patterns rich in movement using tie-dye techniques. See recipes on pages 70, 71, 75, 76, 77, 78, 84, 85, 86, 92, 94, 97, 105, 108.

See recipes on pages 70, 71, 75, 76, 77, 78, 84, 85, 86, 92, 94, 97, 105, 108.

Equipment

Safety clothing

Rubber bands or other binding material such as cotton thread, yarn or wire

Keys, marbles or any other small, indestructible object

Glass or metal dye pots for mixing

Metal dye container

Spatula

Tongs

Basic recipe for approx. 1sq m (9sq ft) fine cotton weighing 100g (4oz)

2g (⅓tsp) fuchsia direct dye powder dissolved in 100ml (½ cup) hot water

25g (1oz) household salt

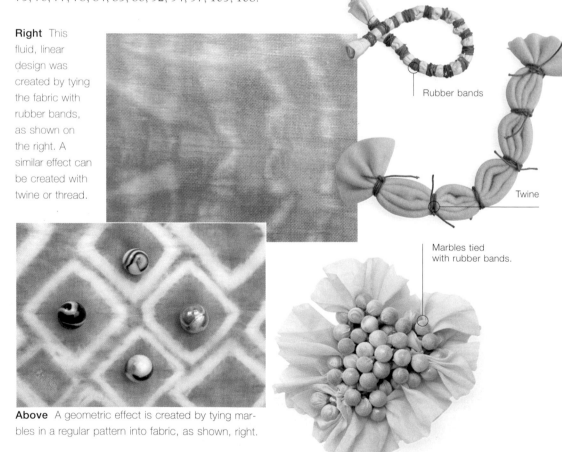

Right This fluid, linear design was created by tying the fabric with rubber bands, as shown on the right. A similar effect can be created with twine or thread.

Rubber bands

Twine

Marbles tied with rubber bands.

Above A geometric effect is created by tying marbles in a regular pattern into fabric, as shown, right.

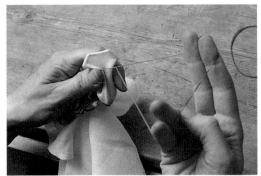

1 Wrap the washed and dried fabric around your chosen object and secure in place by winding rubber bands around it. Note that different objects give different patterns – here I have used keys.

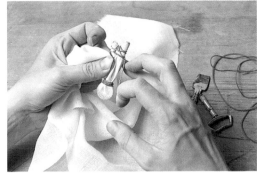

2 Continue to wind the rubber bands round the object until secure. For a different effect, experiment with button thread, raffia, or wire, always securing tightly to prevent the dye penetrating unwanted areas.

4 When the desired colour is reached, rinse well in cold water. Now remove the rubber bands and keys to reveal the pattern.

3 Fill a dye container with cold water and heat until hand warm. Add the dissolved dye and the fabric. Slowly raise the temperature to 80°C (176°F), or just below boiling point, and as it rises, add the salt. Dye for 45 minutes, stirring regularly. Check the colour by lifting a corner of the fabric and squeezing it as dry as possible.

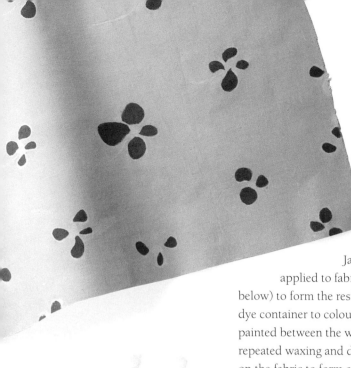

Batik

Practised for over 2,000 years across South Asia, batik is a traditional method of patterning fabric using wax as a resist. Many different batik patterning techniques are still in use today, such as the fine-dot style of line work from Java. In the batik technique, hot liquid wax is applied to fabric using a tool known as a tjanting (see below) to form the resist pattern. Either the fabric is dipped in a dye container to colour the unwaxed areas or dye colours are painted between the waxed areas to form a coloured pattern. By repeated waxing and dipping, you can build up a range of colours on the fabric to form a multi-coloured design. One of the most exciting aspects of batik is adding the layers of colour and pattern, which are only revealed after you remove all the wax from your fabric at the end. Once you have mastered the basic technique, using tjanting tools readily available from specialist craft stores, you can make your own tools to create a linear wax resist pattern by bending and shaping fine wire. This design can also be built up in layers to add depth and detail to your fabric.

Paraffin wax

Equipment

Safety clothing
Plastic dye pots for mixing
One small and one large
    pan or bain-marie
Spatula
Tjanting tools
Paintbrush
Craft knife and palette knife
Brown paper and iron

Basic recipe for approx.
1 sq m (9sq ft) cotton
weighing 100 g (4oz)

100g (4oz) beeswax
100g (4oz) paraffin wax
100g (4oz) ready mixed
    pink pigment dye colour
8g (1¾tsp) yellow cold-water
    reactive dye dissolved in
    100ml (½ cup) hot water
40g (1½oz) household salt
10g (2tsp) sodium carbonate

Dyeing waxed fabric

Once you have applied the wax and allowed it to dry, there are a number of possibilities for dyeing. Note that you need to ensure that the wax has penetrated the fabric well, otherwise the dye will soak through the fabric and affect your design. To prevent this, use fine fabrics such as organdie cotton or silk habotai, or batik the design onto both sides of the fabric. You can use a cold-water dye recipe (see pages 72 and 79), or if you are painting over or between waxed areas, use pigment colours (see pages 112 and 123), as these can easily be fixed at the same time as removing the wax residue. Take care if using other recipes to decorate or colour the fabric because the wax can easily crack when folded or rolled too much.

Tjanting tools

1 Put the beeswax and paraffin wax in a pan and then place in a pan of water over low heat and melt. This mix is ideal as beeswax is soft and not easy to remove, while paraffin wax is harder and easy to use.

2 Secure your fabric tightly to an old picture-frame, box, or printing table with pins. Fill the tjanting with wax and draw your pattern. Hold a piece of paper under the tjanting to protect the fabric from wax drips.

3 When all the wax outlines are drawn, leave to dry. Then use a paintbrush to fill in the outlines with the ready-made pigment dye colours.

4 Once dry, apply more wax over the painted areas using the tjanting tool. This will protect your design from becoming discoloured when it is placed in the dye container.

5 If you have made a mistake or applied too much wax, you can scrape off any excess wax with a craft knife, taking great care not to damage the fabric.

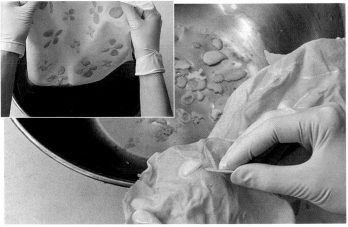

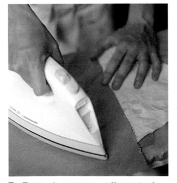

6 To colour the fabric afterwards, fill the dye container with cold water and add the dissolved yellow cold-water reactive dye colour powder. Mix the salt and sodium carbonate together and add in two stages. Stirring occasionally, allow to dye for 45 minutes to 1 hour or until the desired colour is reached. Rinse well and leave to dry.

7 Once dry, scrape off most of the wax using a palette knife. To remove stubborn wax, place a sheet of brown paper over the fabric and iron with a hot iron. The brown paper will soak up the remaining wax and the ironing will fix the dye.

Stencilling

The technique of stencilling, whereby dye or a resist paste is applied to the cut-out portion of a stencil, is an early form of screen-printing.

Stencils can be used in a variety of ways: you can build up a coloured design by cutting multiples of stencils to make up each coloured area or you can re-use the same stencil as a repeat motif to build up a design pattern across your fabric.

Ready-cut acetate stencils, available from craft outlets and specialist stencil stores, can also be used. You just need to clean and dry the stencil well before using it with a different dye. You can also cut your own stencils from newspaper, wax paper or acetate for a more personal touch.

Stencil materials

To cut your own stencils you will need a suitable cutting surface such as a cutting mat or a piece of thick cardboard and a sharp craft knife. More specialist tools are also available, such as hot wire tools for acetate stencils and a double-bladed scalpel (xacto knife) for cutting fine line areas. When cutting out stencils, always remember to include design "bridges", or small joining sections of stencil, so that the stencil stays in one piece.

Although paper stencils are not re-usable, it is worth experimenting with them, either on their own or with a blank silkscreen technique (see page 50), as they are a quick and economical way of decorating fabric.

If you want to create a fine detailed pattern using stencils, heat-fix paper is a good material to use. Commonly used for making dress patterns and available from dressmaking suppliers, this paper has a layer of adhesive on one side so that the stencil can be stuck to your fabric with no risk of the dye getting underneath and breaking down your design. First cut your stencil out of the paper and then very lightly iron the paper down on to the fabric, where it will stick. Be careful not to press too hard or the paper will stick too firmly and will require soaking off.

Equipment

Safety clothing

Glass or metal dye pots with lids for mixing

Cutting surface and craft knife

Acetate sheet and masking tape

Stippling brush or stencil brush

Iron

Basic recipe for approx. 1sq m (9sq ft) heavy viscose

3 x 100g (4oz) ready-mixed pigment dye colours: green, brown and gold

Above Transfer your design to paper or photocopy it onto matt film (as shown above) to provide an invaluable guide to your stencil cutting.

1 Place a cutting mat or piece of thick cardboard on a firm surface. Tape your design to the cutting mat and then tape the acetate on top to prevent it slipping.

2 Taking great care not to cut yourself, cut out the stencil design using a craft knife with a sharp blade. Be very careful not to cut through the original design. However, if you do cut an area by mistake, you can simply tape it back onto the stencil without damaging the design.

3 Now place the cut stencil on the fabric and secure with spray mount or masking tape. Using a stencil brush, stippling brush or sponge, apply the dye through the stencil. Always brush toward the centre of the stencil to avoid the dye leaking underneath and spoiling your design.

4 You can build up several colours within the one stencil area to produce a more colourful effect. Here I have applied green, gold and brown dye colours. Allow each stencilled area to dry thoroughly before moving on to the next. If you are planning a large piece, it is a good idea to mark out the fabric with registration marks (see page 36) before you start.

5 When you have finished applying all the dye pigment colours, allow to dry. Always remember to wash your brushes in water immediately after use. Finally, using a hot iron, press the back of the fabric carefully for about 5 minutes to fix the dye.

Block printing

Block printing has been used as a method of transferring writing and images onto paper and fabric for centuries. It is still widely used in India as a technique for decorating fabrics, and today's block-printed fabrics can be just as delicate and colourful as the 18th- and 19th-century calicos, chintzes and toile de Jouy that India exported all over the world. Blocks from the 19th century are still used by small wallpaper and textile companies today, and you can sometimes come across these useful pin blocks (as shown on the right) in antique markets and stores. Although you may only find one block out of a set of six or eight that made up the full colour design, it is still worth printing with these old blocks, because their attention to detail is very hard to reproduce with modern blocks. See block-printing recipes on pages 147, 148 and 153.

antique pin block

Making a simple block

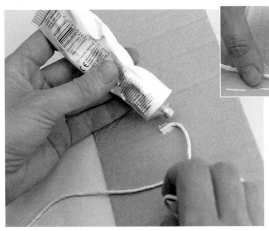

1 Glue thick string to the centre of a small piece of thick card to form a raised spiral motif.

2 Coat the entire block with two coats of an oil-based lacquer or varnish and leave to dry.

3 Fold and tape the ends of the card to make a handle.

Equipment

Safety clothing
Piece of thick cardboard
   7 x 20cm (3 x 8in)
Piece of string
White craft glue
Oil-based lacquer or varnish
Glass or plastic dye pots with
lids for mixing and storing
Paintbrush
Glass or metal dye pot
Iron

Basic recipe for approx. 1sq m (9sq ft) fine cotton weighing 100g (4oz)

100g (4oz) ready-mixed
   pigment dye colour
2g (⅓tsp) light blue direct-
   dye powder dissolved in
   100ml (½ cup) hot water
25g (1oz) household salt

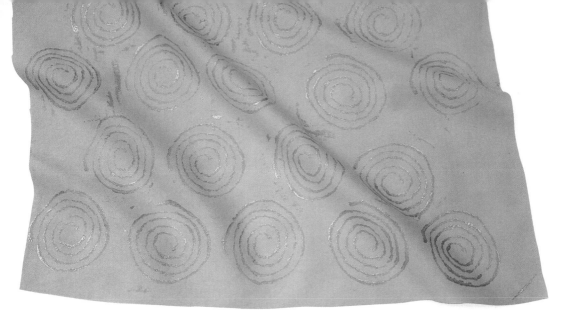

Using printing blocks

1 Lightly paint the raised motif with an even coat of the mixed pigment dye paste. The motif needs to absorb the dye colour, but try to avoid getting too much of it on the cardboard.

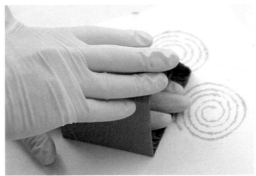

2 Dab the block onto a piece of spare, thick fabric to remove any excess dye. Now print the spiral onto your fabric, re-coating the block with dye when necessary. Leave to dry and then iron to fix the dye.

3 To colour the fabric, fill a dye container with warm water and add the dissolved light blue direct dye. Add the fabric, and raise the temperature to 80°C (176°F), or just below boiling, while adding the salt. Dye for 30 to 45 minutes, stirring occasionally. Remove from the container, rinse well and allow to dry.

Screenprinting

Screenprinting is an extremely versatile way of putting patterns onto fabric. Stencils and gum and wax resists (see pages 54–55) can be used to form the image to be printed. In the technique, dye paste is pushed evenly and smoothly through the screen's mesh with a rubber squeegee. Most of the recipes using dye pastes in this book can be used with a screen, although the paste must be of the consistency of double cream to print effectively. If necessary, add more water or thickening binder. Always practise first on spare fabric, printing quickly before the paste dries on the screen.

Specialist squeegees and small inexpensive screens for general use are available from craft stores. Alternatively, you can use a window-cleaning squeegee and make your own screen (see below).

Making a screen

Equipment

Small wooden frame, such as an old picture frame or artists' stretcher bars

Polyester screen mesh for general fabric printing or polyester net curtaining or organza fabric

Staple gun and staples

Strips of thick card

Tape

Scissors

1 Stretch the mesh tightly and evenly across the wooden frame. Attach securely using a staple gun, working from the centre of each side out to the corners.

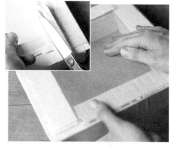

2 Cut off any excess fabric. Tighten the mesh by pushing strips of thick card between the mesh and frame. Finally, tape the back of the screen to seal.

Simple screenprinting technique

1 Tape a reservoir at one end of the screen so that the dye does not run out while printing. Pour dye paste into the reservoir.

2 Hold the frame with one hand, and with the other, use the squeegee to pull the dye firmly through the screen to the fabric.

3 After printing, pour any excess paste back into the pot ready to use again. Clean the screen and squeegee in cold running water.

Stencilling with a silkscreen

1 Cut a stencil out of newsprint (see page 46), leaving plenty of spare paper around the design.

2 Using masking tape, carefully tape the cut newsprint stencil to the back (underside) of the screen. The stencil should be positioned as centrally as possible on the screen.

3 Hold the screen up to the light to check the position of the stencil. Pour the ready-mixed pigment colour into the reservoir. It should be like double cream in consistency.

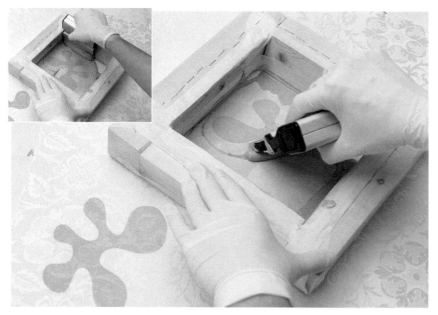

4 With a squeegee, pull the paste firmly across the screen 2 to 4 times. By varying the angle of the squeegee, you can apply more or less paste. The stencil will allow you to do repeated prints with one colour, covering the fabric quickly. Fix the colour with a hot iron. After printing, throw away the stencil and wash the squeegee and screen immediately in cold water.

Monoprinting

You can paint liquid fabric dyes directly onto a silkscreen and then transfer this design onto fabric using clear printing paste and a squeegee. This technique is often used by textile designers, because it allows them to try a wide range of designs and colours quickly on fabric without the costly and time-consuming methods of normal silkscreen production. It is also used to produce painterly effects on fabric – because you are working on the mesh and not directly on the fabric, you can change elements of the design if necessary.

Dyes that can be painted directly onto a screen include acid dye paste for silk (see recipe on page 89) and reactive dye paste for cotton, linen and viscose (see recipe on page 79). The clear paste that allows you to transfer the painted image on the screen to fabric is made by mixing the rest of the recipe ingredients.

(see recipe on page 89)
(see recipe on page 79)

Equipment

Safety clothing

Glass or plastic dye pots for mixing and storing

Metal dye pots

Electric hand-mixer or blender

Spatula for mixing

Paintbrushes and droppers

Blank silkscreen and squeegee

Kitchen foil

Small steamer

Basic recipe for approx. 1sq m (9sq ft) cotton

30g (1¼oz) sodium alginate thickener

300ml (1⅓ cups) warm water

75g (2¾oz) urea dissolved in 150ml (⅔cup) hot water

8g (1¾tsp) washing soda

15ml (3tsp) wetting agent

15g (½oz) sodium carbonate or sodium bicarbonate dissolved in 120ml (½ cup) cold water

10g (2tsp) reactive dye powder colour dissolved in 50ml (¼ cup) boiling water

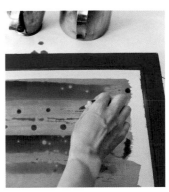

1 In a plastic pot, mix the sodium alginate thickener with the warm water using an electric hand-mixer. Add the dissolved urea, washing soda, wetting agent and the dissolved sodium carbonate. Mix well with a spatula.

2 In a metal pot, make up each colour required by dissolving the reactive dye powder colour in boiling water. Now, using a paintbrush, paint your design onto the back of the silkscreen using the dissolved dye colour.

3 Blend the colours into each other while the dyes are still wet to create a softer effect. Try adding drops of complementary colours with a small dropper for additional pattern effects.

4 With the addition of more colours, the design takes on a more fluid and organic shape. When finished, leave the screen to dry flat. Now pin or tape your fabric to the printing table.

5 Tape the edges of the back of the screen to prevent excess paste getting onto the fabric.

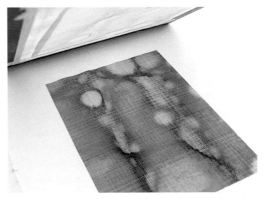

6 Turn the silkscreen over and place over the fabric. Pour the clear printing paste mixed in step 1 at one end of the screen. Now, using a squeegee, pull the paste firmly once or twice across the screen to print the design onto the fabric.

7 Raise the screen to reveal the design transferred to the fabric. Scrape off any excess paste and wash the screen and squeegee in cold running water. Leave the fabric to dry and follow the instructions for processing the fabric detailed on page 113.

Wax printing

It is possible to use wax and gum arabic to make up a silkscreen for monoprinting. For example, you can use a softened wax crayon to draw a design onto the screen. The screen is then coated with gum arabic and the wax is removed; a positive image ready to print will be revealed. The advantage of this technique, known as glue and touché printing, is that the design you draw is the one you will print, rather than being the negative resist as in the other gum arabic and wax techniques described here.

Gum arabic can also be used to paint a resist pattern, this time onto the back of the silkscreen (the side that does not come into contact with the squeegee). Once the gum arabic has dried, the silk

Glue and touché printing

1 Soften an oil-based wax crayon by wrapping in foil and soaking in hot water for a few minutes.

Equipment	Basic recipe for approx. 1sq m (9sq ft) viscose felt
Safety clothing	
Soft oil-based wax crayon	200g (7oz) ready-mixed green pigment dye colour
Kitchen foil	
Glass pot and hot water	100ml (½ cup) liquid gum arabic
Spatula	
Silkscreen and squeegee	150ml (⅔ cup) white spirit or turpentine
Soft rags	
Iron	

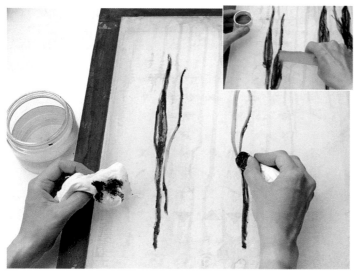

2 Draw your design onto the back of the screen with the softened wax crayon and leave to dry. Using a piece of card, apply a thin layer of gum arabic over the back of the screen up to the edges and allow to dry.

3 Wearing safety clothing, firmly rub both sides of the screen at the same time with soft rags soaked in white spirit or turpentine. The wax will be removed, revealing the design. Once dry, use ready-mixed pigment dye to screenprint the design (see page 50). Allow to dry and iron to fix.

screen is ready to use, but note that the gum arabic will wash out when you wash the silkscreen to remove excess paste after printing.

Liquid wax, such as that used in the batik technique on page 44, can also be used in a similar way to make a negative resist pattern on the back of the silkscreen. Try painting or using a tjanting tool to create your design. When cooled and dried, the waxed silkscreen can be used to screenprint the design onto the fabric using dye pastes.

Always remember to wash the waxed silkscreen and squeegee immediately after use in plenty of cold running water and the wax design will remain on the screen ready for you to use again. To remove the wax, first soak the silkscreen in boiling water and then wash thoroughly in hot running water.

Gummed wax printing

1 Trace your design onto the silkscreen using a pencil. Here, gingko leaves are my inspiration.

Equipment	Basic recipe for approx. 1sq m (9sq ft) viscose felt
Safety clothing	200g (7oz) ready-mixed pigment dye colour
Pencil and paintbrush	
Silkscreen, squeegee	
Pins and tape	100ml (½ cup) liquid gum arabic
Glass or plastic dye pot for mixing	
Spatula	
Iron	

2 Using a paintbrush, paint the areas of the design you do not wish to print with gum arabic. Remember to work on the back of the silkscreen. Tape the edges of the screen. While waiting for the gum arabic to dry, pin out the fabric onto the printing table.

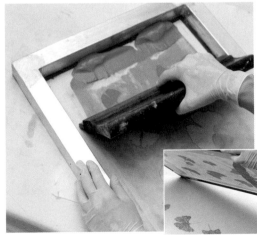

3 Pull the ready-mixed dye pigment colour across the screen with a squeegee to print the design. Lift the screen to reveal the design and allow to dry. Wash the screen and squeegee in cold running water. Finally, fix the dye colour with a hot iron.

Devoré

Equipment

Safety clothing

Glass or plastic dye pots with lids for mixing and storing

Electric hand-mixer or blender

Spatula

Pins or tape

Ready-cut acetate stencil

Spray glue

Sponge

Iron

Basic recipe for approx. 1sq m (9sq ft) silk–viscose velvet

30g (1¼oz) modified guar gum

250ml (1 cup) warm water

10ml (2tsp) glycerine

20g (¾oz) tartaric acid

80g (3 oz) aluminium sulphate

100ml (½ cup) cold water

In the devoré technique, a chemical paste and heat are used to destroy or burn away one of the fibres in a mixed-fibre fabric. The most common type of devoré fabric is made using silk-viscose velvet. Here the viscose pile is removed, leaving the silk chiffon background in place to create a design within the fabric. This technique can also be applied to other mixed-fibre types, such as polyester-cotton mixes and silk-viscose satin.

There are two kinds of devoré paste: acid devoré paste described here, which removes cellulose fibres such as cotton; and alkali devoré paste, used in the recipe on page 125, which removes protein fibres such as wool. Note that the devoré pastes must be handled with care at all times. Always wear protective gloves, an apron and a respirator when handling the pastes. Remember to store them in dry, air-tight containers out of the reach of children.

In the technique shown here, the devoré paste is applied using a stencil, but you can also paint or silkscreen the design onto the fabric. Note that the paste is always applied to the back of the fabric. This technique is used in the recipes on pages 100, 125, and 137.

Viscose fibres rubbed away from chiffon after applying the devoré technique.

1 Wearing safety clothing, mix the modified guar gum and warm water using an electric hand-mixer or blender. Place in a plastic pot and then add all the other ingredients and mix well.

2 Pin or tape the velvet, pile-side down, to the work surface. Lightly spray the ready-cut stencil with spray mount, wiping away any excess glue, and then place the stencil on the fabric.

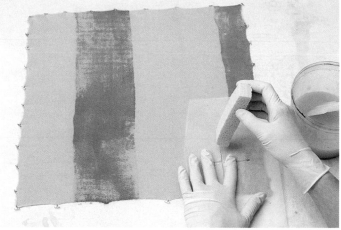

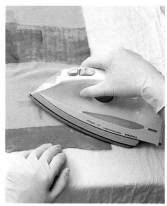

3 Using the sponge, paint the devoré paste mixed in step 1 evenly through the stencil onto the fabric. Take care not to move the stencil as you apply the paste to prevent any chemicals spreading onto unwanted areas. Applying too much paste can destroy the fabric. Repeat the process for each design motif to be devoréd, and then allow to dry.

4 Using a hot iron, press the back of the fabric firmly for about 30 seconds to 1 minute. While ironing, be very careful to ensure that the heat of the iron does not destroy the fabric by burning completely through the fibres.

5 When the patterned area turns slightly brown, stop ironing and turn the fabric over so that the pile is facing upwards. Wearing safety clothing, rub the design area with your fingertips to remove the pile.

6 Continue rubbing the fabric until the fabric feels stiff and all the pile has been removed. Finally, wash the fabric in mild detergent to remove the stiffness (the remains of the modified guar gum) and leave to dry.

Colour stripping

Colour stripping is the process of using chemicals to remove colour from a piece of previously dyed fabric. Sometimes referred to as discharge, this technique produces a white design on a coloured background. You can also add colouring dyes to the chemicals and remove and replace the colour in the design at the same time in a process known as illuminating. Note that not all synthetic dyestuffs are dischargeable (removable), so always do a test piece first. Colour stripping and illuminating can be used with other techniques or recipes to produce a variety of patterned fabrics (see recipes on pages 147, 152 and 153.).

Depending on fabric type, various stripping agents are used. There is great scope for experimenting with this technique. Subtle tonal effects can be achieved by decreasing the amount of stripping agent and applying it lightly. Dyeing the fabric first, either with fully dischargeable dyes or dyes that will not discharge, will create unusual colour effects.

Equipment
Safety clothing

Glass or plastic dye pots with lids for mixing and storing

Electric or hand whisk or blender

Clean newsprint

Pins and masking tape

Paintbrush

Kitchen foil

Wok or pressure cooker for steaming

Basic recipe for approx. 1 sq m (9sq ft) silk
30g (1¼oz) modified guar gum mixed with 250ml (1 cup) warm water

50g (1¾oz) zinc formaldehyde sulphoxylate (reducing agent)

20ml (4tsp) glycerine

180ml (⅔cup) cold water

This technique involves the use of harmful chemicals which must be handled with care at all times. Always wear protective gloves, an apron and a respirator when handling the chemicals and store them in dry, air-tight containers out of the reach of children.

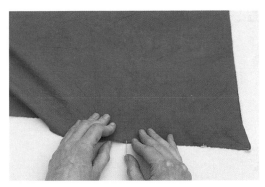

1 Wearing safety clothing, put the mixed modified guar gum into a plastic pot and add the reducing agent, glycerine and cold water. Stir well until an even paste is formed.

2 Spread a thin layer of gum arabic on your work table and when dry, iron down a backing cloth. Pin the fabric to be decorated firmly to this cloth so that it does not move while you are working on it.

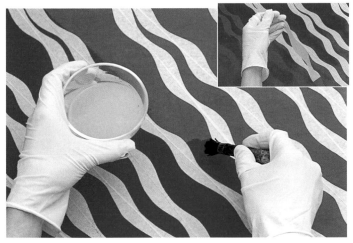

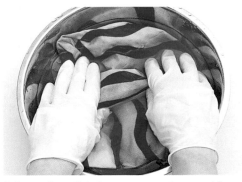

3 Cut and apply masking tape across all of the fabric to form a pattern. Here I have cut the tape randomly to form a design of wavy lines. Now, using a paintbrush, apply the colour stripping paste mixed in step 1 to the fabric between the tape. Allow to dry, but do not leave overnight before starting step 4.

4 Unpin the fabric from the table, place clean newsprint paper under the fabric and roll into a loose tube shape so that the fabric does not come into contact with itself, thus preventing marking off. Loosely wrap this in kitchen foil, sealing the edges well so that water cannot enter.

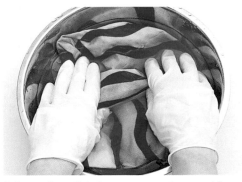

5 Place the foil parcel on a rack above the water in the steamer to prevent water from coming into contact with the parcel. Allow to steam for 10 minutes, after which time the paste will have removed the colour.

6 In a well-ventilated area, remove the parcel from the steamer with care, and leave to cool. Wash first in cold running water, then in warm water with a little mild washing powder. Allow to dry and then iron.

Working with yarn

Dyeing yarn is very similar to dyeing fabric, although extra care must be taken to raise the temperature slowly and not to overheat the yarn when dyeing wool and silk. Wool yarn will easily felt when boiled and be of no use for further work. Silk yarn will also be harder to work with and break easily if overheated. Note, however, that polyester requires high temperatures to dye successfully.

The recipes in the vat-dyeing section of this book, using both natural and synthetic dyes, can all be used to dye yarn as well as fabric. Check carefully what type of yarn you are dyeing so that you choose the appropriate dyestuff.

Cones of yarn

Hanking yarn

1 To dye yarn successfully, you will need to hank the yarn. Use the back of a chair to make a hank from a ball or cone of yarn.

2 Wrap the yarn around the chair to form the hank, making each hank about 100g (4oz). Tie the ends together when finished.

3 Place additional loose ties throughout the hank and tie the ends together so the hank is held together in three or four places.

Round a friend's hands
Try winding a yarn round a friend's outstretched hands. Tie the loose ends together and add loose ties in the same way as shown above.

Round your arm First wind the start of the yarn round your thumb a few times to hold it in place. Then wind between your hand and elbow. When finished, remove and add ties as above.

Above In ikat weaving, the warp threads that make up the length of the fabric are decorated with a pattern before the weft threads, or those that go across the fabric, are added.

As with fabric, the amount of dye you need is controlled by the amount of yarn you are dyeing and the required strength of colour.

Undyed yarn can be purchased in many different forms – in a ball, on a cone or as hanks. For successful dyeing, the yarn must be wound into hanks. Making the hanks about 100g (4oz) in weight will help to ensure even pick-up of the dye and keep your hank tangle-free. Before dyeing, always remember to wash the yarn first as you do with fabric, taking care not to tangle the hanks.

Once you have mastered the basic techniques, you can try mixing the colours in a hank by tie-dyeing sections, see recipes on pages 78, 105 and 108. Or use the recipe on page 102 for a striking two-colour effect.

Hanks of dyed woollen yarn

Dyed mohair yarn wound into a ball

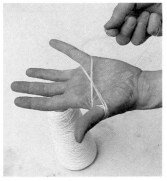

Round your hand For fine yarn or small hanks, wind round your hand. Wind the starting thread around the thumb a few times to hold in place and tie as before.

Round a sponge Fine yarn can also be wound round a sponge. Add ties to hold the yarn together when dyeing and then remove the sponge when washing the hank.

Dyeing mixed yarns

S ome of the most unusual and interesting effects can be
achieved by dyeing different types of yarn, such as wool and
silk, or wool, silk and viscose, in the same container. This is
because dye powders vary in their affinity for each type of fibre so
that different yarns pick up the dye colour in different ways.

Using synthetic dyes to dye mixed yarn will produce intriguing
results. For example, if you dye wool, silk and nylon yarn with red
acid dye, it will produce shades of deep, strong red on the wool
and silk, and a shade of pink on the nylon. See recipe on page 89
for dyeing mixed fibres with acid dyes.

Natural dyes will also produce a wide range of tones on mixed
fibres. Almost all the natural dye recipes in the vat-dyeing section
of this book can be used on natural cotton, linen, silk and wool
yarns. Although they usually need to be mordanted in separate
mordanting baths (see page 24), when you start dyeing you can
place all these different yarn types into one natural dye container to
create an unusual colour mix in your yarn. Different tones can also
be achieved by mixing non-mordanted yarns with mordanted
yarns. However, note that the non-mordanted yarns will fade at a
quicker rate than the mordanted yarns.

Note also that dyeing different weights, thicknesses, and types
of the same yarn with other synthetic dyes will produce a multi-
toned range of colours (see recipes on pages 90 and 95).

1 Place all the yarns you want to dye together. Make a hank by holding one end of the yarn under your thumb and winding the yarn between your open palm and bent arm.

2 Bend a wire coathanger upwards at both ends so that you can use it as a handle for holding and moving the yarn in the dye container.

3 Fill a dye container with water and add the dissolved acetic acid and dissolved acid dye powder colour. Raise the temperature slowly to 80°C (176°F), or just below boiling point, and place the yarn on its hanger in the dye for 45 minutes.

4 Using the hanger, move the yarn frequently in the dye container to ensure that the dye is distributed evenly over the yarn. To check the colour, raise the yarn from the dye and, holding a small part of the yarn between your fingertips, squeeze out the excess dye. The resulting colour will give you a good idea of whether the required colour has been obtained.

5 When finished, rinse the yarn well in cold running water until the water runs clear. When fully rinsed, the yarn will be full of knots and tangles. Before you can use the yarn, you will need to untangle it.

6 Hold the yarn between both hands. Move your hands quickly together and then out again to bang out all the knots and tangles. Gradually a smooth hank of yarn will be formed.

recipes

The recipes that follow will guide you in easy stages through each of the colouring and decorating techniques and their effects. By using all the symbols provided throughout the recipe section you will be able to quickly and easily decide which recipe you'd like to use. With practice, you can use more than one recipe on fabric to create amazing textiles.

Safety first

Colouring and decorating fabrics requires the use of a variety of chemicals ranging from common household store cupboard ingredients to specialist chemical supplies. These chemicals vary in the potential harm they can cause, and although small amounts used infrequently will cause little damage, it is a good idea to get into the habit of taking care at all times when handling these substances. Before starting any of the recipes, check you are wearing the correct safety clothing. Always read through the recipe first and check whether there are any special safety requirements and always follow these warnings carefully. If in any doubt as to the correct method of handling a chemical or the appropriate safety clothing, always refer to the safety sheet supplied with all chemicals by the manufacturers. If you treat chemical ingredients with respect and caution, you will be able to use them safely and enjoyably.

Handling dye powders

If you are required to mix dye powder colours, always wear a face mask and mix the powders in a well-ventilated area with no draught or breeze to avoid inhaling the powders and to prevent the powders dispersing.

Handling liquid chemicals

When handling liquid dyes and chemicals, be extra careful to ensure no splashing occurs. Wear safety goggles to protect your eyes but if any does come into contact with your skin or eyes, irrigate immediately with water and seek further medical advice immediately.

Storing dyeing ingredients

It is extremely important to store all dyes and chemicals safely in airtight containers, labelled clearly with the contents and the date mixed. Keep all dyes and chemicals in a safe, dry place away from cooking areas and safely out of the reach of children, pets and other members of the

Mixing chemicals Always wear the appropriate safety clothing as stated in the recipes when mixing any chemicals.

household. For storage and usage advice of individual chemicals, check the safety sheet which is supplied as a legal requirement with all chemicals.

> **In case of an accident** If any chemical comes into contact with your skin or eyes, wash immediately with water and seek further medical advice if necessary. Take along the safety sheet supplied with the chemicals as it will help your doctor understand the precise composition of the chemical you have been using. Note that some people can get an allergic reaction to some of the dyes or chemicals used in these recipes. If you think you are experiencing a reaction to any chemical, consult your doctor immediately.

What the symbols mean

Each recipe is accompanied by a colour key and a set of symbols that answer many of the questions that you will have before starting a project. The symbols tell you what fabric and dye to use, how to apply and fix the dye, the safety precautions you will need and the level of difficulty.

Which fabric?

The coloured strips down the outside of each recipe page indicate the fabric type – cotton, linen, silk, wool, viscose, nylon, polyester and mixed fibres – that is suitable for the recipe.

What safety precautions do I need to take?

The symbol of an apron indicates the type of safety precautions that you will need to take to complete the recipe successfully. The apron colours indicate three levels of precaution.

Completely safe A blue apron indicates that the recipe uses no dangerous chemicals. However, basic safety clothing – an apron and protective gloves – is always advisable.

Handle with care A violet apron indicates that special care should be taken when handling the dyes and chemicals in the recipe. Safety clothing should be worn at all times.

Dangerous A red apron indicates that the recipe requires the use of dangerous chemicals such as acid or powder dyes. Wear goggles and a safety mask as well as an apron and gloves at all times.

How difficult are the recipes?

The symbol of a protective glove indicates the level of expertise required to complete the recipe successfully. The glove colours indicate three levels of difficulty.

Basic The green outline of a glove indicates that the recipe is suitable for anyone who is a complete beginner to dyeing. Many natural dye recipes carry this symbol.

Intermediate The light green glove indicates that the recipe is of medium difficulty and is suitable for those with some experience and knowledge of dyeing and decorating fabric.

Advanced The dark green glove indicates that the method in the recipe is quite difficult and requires a greater level of expertise than the other recipes in the book.

What kind of dye does the recipe require?

The symbols of a chemical flask and a leaf tell you whether the recipe requires the use of natural or synthetic dyes.

Synthetic dyes required

Natural dyes required

How do I apply the dye?

The symbols below tell you about the method that is used to apply the dye in each recipe. Dyes may be applied in a vat, painted or printed onto fabric.

Vat dyeing The bucket tells you that a vat is required for immersion dyeing.

Painting The brush tells you that the dye must be brushed or rolled onto the fabric.

Printing The block tells you that the dye is printed onto the fabric.

How is the fabric processed?

The symbols below tell you how the dye is fixed onto the fabric in each recipe. Some simple recipes may require only a hot iron, while others may require the use of a steamer to fix the dye.

40°-80°C
(104°-176°F)

Heat The thermometer tells you what temperatures are required to fix the dye.

3 mins

Hot iron The iron tells you how long to press the fabric to fix the dye.

Hot air This symbol indicates that you need to use a hair-dryer to fix the dye.

Steam The vapour cloud indicates that you will need a steamer to fix the dye.

Chemical reaction to air The sun symbol indicates that the dye is fixed in the open air.

4-5 hrs

Processing time The clock indicates the amount of time it will take to complete the recipe.

vat dyeing

This section describes exciting ways of colouring fabric in dye vats. Many recipes use natural dyes from berries or leaves in the garden. All recipes are for 100g (4oz) of dry fabric or yarn unless otherwise stated.

3½hrs   boil

Brazilwood shibori

B razilwood dyestuff, obtained from the heartwood of various species of brazilwood trees, produces a strong red colour that has been used for centuries by dyers throughout the world. Using a variation of the Japanese shibori technique, this pattern is created by sewing running stitch in strong thread to form a resist, with the result that a strong stripe of the fabric stays white.

You will need
- Safety clothing
- Dye container
- Needle and strong thread
- Glass or metal dye pots for mixing
- Spatula and tongs
- Strainer
- Iron

Ingredients
- 7g (1½tsp) alum
- 7g (1½tsp) cream of tartar
- 150ml (⅔ cup) warm water
- 500ml (2 cups) hot water
- 200g (7oz) brazilwood chips

1 Wash your fabric in a mild detergent, rinse and dry.

2 Using a needle and strong thread, sew a running stitch across the fabric at regular intervals, leaving a loose end to the row. Pull up each of these ends tightly to gather the fabric into a narrow strip and tie off very tightly to form the resist pattern.

3 Wearing safety clothing throughout, next mordant the fabric to improve absorption and to prevent the colour from fading over time, following the instructions on page 24.

4 Pour 500ml (2 cups) hot water into a glass or metal dye-mixing pot, and add the brazilwood chips. Bring to the boil and simmer for 30 to 45 minutes. Allow to cool and then strain to remove the brazilwood chips.

5 Place the well-rinsed, mordanted fabric in a dye container and add enough cold water to cover the fabric. Add the brazilwood liquid and bring slowly to the boil over a 30-minute period and then allow to simmer for 1 hour. Stir at regular intervals to distribute the dye evenly over the fabric. If necessary, add some more water to keep the fabric covered.

6 Check the colour by rinsing a corner of the fabric under cold water and ironing dry. Remember that wet fabric may dry to a different shade and you may need to check a few times to get the strength of colour you want.

7 Allow to cool in the dye container. Remove the fabric and rinse well under cold running water and then again in warm water with a little mild detergent. Now you can remove all the threads to release the fabric. Rinse again in cold running water and allow to dry thoroughly.

Madder ball

2 days   65°C (149°F)

cotton

linen

silk

wool

Madder, obtained from the plant *Rubia tinctorum*, is one of the most important natural dyes, because it is very light-fast and can be used with a wide variety of fabric types including cotton, linen, silk, and wool. Producing a deep reddish-brown colour, madder is used here on fine wool to create a random pattern.

1 Wash your fabric in a mild detergent, rinse and dry. Roughly ball up the fabric and wrap the strong thread or rubber bands randomly and tightly around the ball of fabric as if it were a ball of string.

2 Wearing safety clothing throughout, next mordant the fabric to improve absorption and to prevent the colour from fading over time, following the instructions on page 24.

3 Fill the dye container with enough warm water to easily cover the fabric. Place the madder root in the container and leave to soak overnight. The following day, add the well-rinsed mordanted fabric to the dye container and raise the temperature slowly over a 30-minute period to about 65°C (149°F). Be careful to raise the temperature slowly to avoid spoiling the colour by overheating. Simmer for 1 to 2 hours, stirring at regular intervals to distribute the dye evenly over the fabric. If necessary, add more water to keep the fabric covered.

4 Check the colour by rinsing a corner of the fabric and ironing dry. Remember that wet fabric may dry to a different shade and you may need to check a few times to get the strength of colour you want.

5 Allow to cool in the dye container overnight. Remove from the container and rinse well under cold running water. Rinse again in warm water with a little mild detergent. Now you can remove the threads or rubber bands to reveal the pattern. Rinse again in cold running water and leave to dry.

Alternative method Madder can also be used cold, but you will probably need to add more madder root to achieve the same intensity of colour.

You will need
- Safety clothing
- Dye container
- Strong thread or rubber bands
- Glass or metal dye pots for mixing
- Spatula and tongs
- Iron

Ingredients
- 7g (1½tsp) alum
- 7g (1½tsp) cream of tartar
- 150ml (⅔ cup) warm water
- 200g (7oz) madder root

cotton

linen

silk

wool

viscose

mixed fibres

1 day   20 mins

Indigo

You will need
- Safety clothing
- Large strong plastic bucket able to hold 10 litres (2 gallons)
- Lid or plastic wrap to cover bucket
- Glass or metal dye pot for mixing
- Spatula and tongs
- Paper towels

Ingredients
- 9 litres (1¾ gallons) water
- 200g (7oz) household salt
- 50g (1¾oz) natural or synthetic indigo powder or grains
- 100ml (½ cup) warm water
- 12g (¼oz) sodium hydroxide solution 72° TW
- 1 litre (4 cups) warm water
- 35g (1⅓oz) sodium hydrosulphite

Indigo is one of the oldest known dyes, with examples of cloth still surviving that were coloured and patterned blue by this plant thousands of years ago. Indigo-bearing plants were grown throughout the world in large quantities, with regional variations in use, name, and quality. The distinctive blue colour is produced by immersing fabric in a container, or vat, of indigo dye for a short time and then allowing it to oxidize in the air. As a cold-water method of dyeing, it lends itself to a vast range of traditional resist techniques. Today, synthetic indigo dye is most commonly used. Whether you use natural or synthetic indigo at home, the resulting colour is extremely strong and lightfast, and definitely worth the lengthy preparations.

Preparing the indigo vat

1 Heat 9 litres (1¼ gallons) water to a temperature of 50°C (120°F). Pour into a plastic bucket, or large container, and add the salt.

2 In a separate glass or metal container, mix the indigo powder or grains (natural or synthetic) and 100ml (½ cup) warm water together to form a paste.

3 Wearing full safety clothing (sodium hydroxide is very caustic), place 1 litre (4 cups) of warm water in another glass or metal container and add the sodium hydroxide. Always add the sodium hydroxide to the water and never the water to the sodium hydroxide. Stir carefully to dissolve thoroughly.

4 Add the sodium hydroxide solution to the large bucket containing the warm water and salt, and stir well.

5 Now add the sodium hydrosulphite to the main solution in the large bucket. Stir gently to mix, but be careful not to agitate while stirring, because air bubbles will form which will prevent the indigo from working properly.

6 Add the indigo paste and again stir gently to mix.

7 Leave the indigo vat to stand for 30 minutes to 1 hour and you will then see a liquid sheen on the surface of the water created by the indigo oxidizing in contact with the air. Using a paper towel, gently soak up and remove this film, cover the indigo vat and leave for a minimum of 2 to 3 hours. Better results will be obtained if the vat is left to stand overnight.

Dyeing with the indigo vat

1 Wash your fabric using a mild detergent to remove any finishes. If you have used a resist technique to pattern the fabric, do not wash it in case you damage the pattern.

2 Check the surface of the indigo vat and remove any excess oxidized indigo with a paper towel. Squeeze out excess water from the fabric and immerse into the vat. Make sure the fabric stays open so that as much of the surface area as possible is in direct contact with the indigo. Gently stir the fabric, making sure it is below the surface at all times to ensure an even colour.

3 The fabric can stay in the vat for 2 to 15 minutes at a time, depending on the strength and freshness of the indigo vat, the type of fabric used, and the depth of colour required. Test on a small strip of fabric first.

4 Remove the fabric from the vat, and hang it up to oxidize in the air and develop its distinctive blue colour. Be sure to spread the fabric out fully so that it can all oxidize. Beware of drips!

5 After about 20 minutes, the indigo blue colour will fully develop. To build up a deep colour, repeat steps 2 and 3 a few times. A stronger blue is obtained by repeated dipping and oxidizing, not by leaving longer in the vat.

6 When you have the required colour, rinse well in cold running water, then wash in warm water with a mild detergent. Finally, rinse in cold water, and leave to dry.

Reusing the indigo vat

Indigo vats can be reused many times, making them an economical and time-saving method of colouring fabric.

1 Always keep the indigo vat covered with a lid or plastic wrap to keep it airtight.

2 If the vat cools down too much – below 20°C (68°F) – warm it up by placing it in another container of hot water.

3 If the vat looks slightly blue rather than yellow-green in colour, add 3 to 5g (½ to 1tsp) of sodium hydrosulphite and stir gently until the vat turns yellow-green again.

4 When the fabric no longer dyes in the indigo vat, the vat is exhausted. To clean the vat, stir the water quickly to oxidize any excess dye and then rinse in cold water.

5hrs **boil**

Green ivy

You will need

- Safety clothing
- Dye container
- Glass or metal dye pots for mixing
- Spatula and tongs
- Strainer
- Iron

Ingredients

- 7g (1½tsp) alum
- 7g (1½tsp) cream of tartar
- 150ml (⅔cup) warm water
- 200g (7oz) chopped ivy leaves
- Cold water
- 500ml (2 cups) hot water

There are just a few plants that will produce the colour green on their own. One of these is ivy, which grows abundantly and is very easy to gather from your garden or from the hedgerow. Used with a mordant, ivy leaves will dye silk a beautiful green colour.

1 Wash your fabric in a mild detergent, rinse and dry.

2 Wearing safety clothing throughout, next mordant the fabric to improve absorption and to prevent the colour from fading over time, following the instructions on page 24.

3 Place 500ml (2 cups) of hot water into a glass or metal dye-mixing pot, add the chopped ivy leaves, and leave to soak for 1 to 2 hours.

4 Bring the soaked ivy leaves to the boil and simmer for 30 to 45 minutes. Allow to cool and then strain to remove the leaves.

5 Place the fabric in the dye container and fill with plenty of cold water to cover the fabric so that it can be moved freely under the water and then add the ivy liquid. Bring slowly to the boil over a 30-minute period and then simmer for 1 hour. Stir at regular intervals to distribute the dye evenly over the fabric. If necessary, add more water to keep the fabric covered.

6 Check the colour by rinsing a corner of the fabric under cold water and ironing dry. Remember that wet fabric often dries to a different shade and you may need to check a few times to get the strength of colour you want.

7 Allow to cool in the dye container and then remove and rinse well under cold running water. Rinse again in warm water with a little mild detergent. Finally, rinse in cold running water and leave to dry.

Walnut twist

2½hrs   boil

silk

wool

Walnut leaves and the green outer husks of walnuts both produce useful natural dyestuffs. William Morris used walnut dye to obtain a good black colour after first dyeing with indigo. The roots or husks of the walnut plant produce a strong plum colour, but this recipe uses walnut leaves to make an intense yellow colour.

1 Wash your fabric in a mild detergent, rinse and dry. Starting with one corner of the fabric, twist the remaining fabric constantly and tightly until you have a long thin piece of fabric. Keep twisting and the fabric will twist up into a small tight knot. Secure this shape by tying the ends tightly with strong thread or rubber bands.

2 Wearing safety clothing throughout, next mordant the fabric to improve absorption and to prevent the colour from fading over time, following the instructions on page 24.

3 Place 500ml (2 cups) of hot water in a glass or metal dye-mixing pot and add the walnut leaves. Bring to the boil and simmer for 30 to 45 minutes. Allow to cool and then strain to remove the walnut leaves.

4 Place the well-rinsed, mordanted fabric in the dyeing container and fill with enough cold water to cover the fabric. Add the walnut liquid and bring slowly to the boil over a 30-minute period and then simmer for 1 hour. Stir at regular intervals to distribute the dye evenly over the fabric. If necessary, add more water to keep the fabric covered.

5 Check the colour by rinsing a corner of the fabric and ironing dry. Remember that wet fabric often dries to a different shade, and you may need to check a few times to get the strength of colour you want.

6 Allow to cool in the dye container. Remove and rinse well under cold running water and then rinse again in warm water with a little mild detergent. Now you can remove the ties to release the fabric and reveal your pattern. Rinse again in cold running water and leave to dry.

> **Alternative colourways** You can use the roots and husks of the walnut plant to obtain a deep plum colour. First grind to a powder and then make up into a paste with hot water. Add in at stage 4 instead of the walnut liquid.

You will need
- Safety clothing
- Dye container
- Strong thread or rubber bands
- Glass or metal dye pots for mixing
- Spatula and tongs
- Strainer
- Iron

Ingredients
- 7g (1½tsp) alum
- 7g (1½tsp) cream of tartar
- 150ml (⅔cups) warm water
- 200g (7oz) walnut leaves
- 500ml (2 cups) hot water

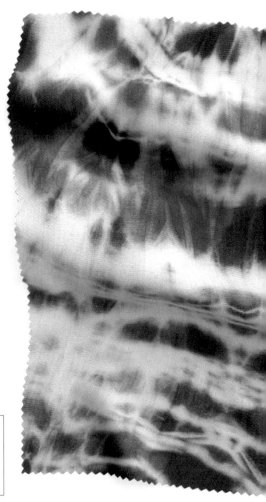

3½hrs   boil

Persian berry

You will need
- Safety clothing
- Dye container
- Beads and sequins
- Strong sewing thread
- Glass or metal dye pots for mixing
- Strainer, spatula and tongs
- Iron

Ingredients
- 7g (1½tsp) alum
- 7g (1½tsp) cream of tartar
- 150ml (⅔ cup) warm water
- 20g (¾oz) Persian berries
- 100ml (½ cup) hot water

B eads and sequins are used here with Persian berries to create a beautiful yellow pattern on wool. Used for centuries to dye yarn and cloth, Persian berry comes from the berries of several species of buckthorn trees. You can also use the bark, although the colours produced will be less intense. Note that if using the bark, a mordant will not be necessary.

1 Wash your fabric in a mild detergent, rinse and dry. Sew the beads and sequins tightly to the fabric in small groups to create a random pattern.

2 Wearing safety clothing throughout, next mordant the fabric to improve absorption and to prevent the colour from fading over time, following the instructions on page 24.

3 Place 100ml (½ cup) of hot water into a glass or metal dye-mixing pot and add the Persian berries. Bring to the boil and simmer for 45 minutes. Allow to cool and then strain to remove the berries.

4 Place the well-rinsed, mordanted fabric in the dye container and add enough cold water to cover the fabric. Add the Persian berry liquid and bring slowly to the boil over a 30-minute period and then simmer for 1 hour. Stir at regular intervals to distribute the dye evenly over the fabric. If necessary, add more water to keep the fabric covered.

5 Check the colour by rinsing a corner of the fabric and ironing dry. Remember that wet fabric often dries to a different shade and you may need to check a few times to get the strength of colour you want.

6 Allow to cool in the dye container. Remove and rinse well under cold running water and then rinse again in warm water with a little mild detergent. Now you can remove all the beads and sequins to reveal the pattern. Finally rinse in cold running water and leave to dry.

Onion skin ribbons

2½hrs   boil

silk

wool

V arious shades ranging from deep orange to a rich rust can be obtained on wool by using common onion skins. This natural dyestuff can produce particularly interesting results when used with a tie-dye technique of ribbons instead of threads. Try using other types of onions, such as red onions, to achieve different shades.

1 Wash your fabric in a mild detergent, rinse and dry. Pick up points of the fabric and bind very tightly with the ribbon so that no fabric shows and no dye colour can get under the ribbon and spoil your design.

2 Wearing safety clothing throughout, next mordant the fabric to improve absorption and to prevent the colour from fading over time, following the instructions on page 24.

3 Place 500ml (2 cups) of hot water in a glass or metal dye-mixing pot and add the onion skins. Bring to the boil and simmer for 30 to 45 minutes. Allow to cool and then strain to remove the onion skins.

4 Place the well rinsed, mordanted fabric in the dyeing container and fill with enough cold water to cover the fabric. Add the onion skin liquid and bring slowly to the boil over a 30-minute period and then allow to simmer for 1 hour. Stir at regular intervals to distribute the dye evenly over the fabric. If necessary, add more water to keep the fabric covered.

5 Check the colour by rinsing a corner of the fabric and ironing dry. Remember that wet fabric often dries to a different shade and you may need to check a few times to get the strength of colour you want.

6 Allow to cool in the dye container. Remove and rinse well under cold running water and then rinse again in warm water with a little mild detergent. Now you can remove the ribbons to release the fabric. Rinse again in cold running water and leave to dry.

You will need
- Safety clothing
- Dye container
- Lengths of ribbon
- Glass or metal dye pots for mixing
- Spatula and tongs
- Strainer
- Iron

Ingredients
- 7g (1½tsp) alum
- 7g (1½tsp) cream of tartar
- 150ml (⅔ cup) warm water
- 80g (3oz) dried onion skins
- 500ml (2 cups) hot water

2hrs 40°-80°C
(104°-176°F)

Two-colour magic

T his intriguing recipe shows you how to produce a two-colour effect on wool with just one dye container. The secret of this technique is to tie-dye the fabric at the mordant stage and then remove the ties at the dyeing stage, thereby producing the two-colour effect. In this recipe, the wool is treated with a chrome mordant before the dyeing stage.

You will need
- Safety clothing
- Strong thread or rubber bands
- Dye container
- Glass or metal dye pots for mixing
- Spatula and tongs
- Iron

Ingredients
- 10g (2tsp) sodium bi-chromate
- 6ml (1¼tsp) formic acid at 85% strength
- 20ml (4tsp) cold water
- 2g (⅓tsp) sodium bisulphate
- 4g (¾tsp) chrome acid dye powder
- 100ml (½ cup) hot water

1 Wash the fabric with a mild detergent to remove any finishes so that the dye will take evenly, then leave to dry. Pick a point in the centre of the fabric and bind tightly with strong thread or rubber bands. Place ties at regular intervals along the resulting bunch of fabric to form the pattern.

2 Fill the dye container with cold water and heat on an electric or gas ring until hand-warm.

3 Wearing safety clothing, place 20ml (4tsp) of cold water in a glass or metal dye-mixing pot and add the formic acid. Now add this solution to the dye container.

4 Add the sodium bi-chromate and the fabric to the dye container and bring rapidly to the boil. Continue to simmer for 45 minutes, taking care not to allow it to boil dry.

5 Carefully add the sodium bisulphate and continue to simmer for another 15 to 20 minutes.

6 Remove the fabric carefully and rinse in warm water with a small amount of mild detergent. Rinse again in cold water and then remove the strong thread or rubber bands.

7 Follow the instructions for acid dyeing on page 89, substituting 4g (¾tsp) of chrome acid dye powder colour for the 2g (⅓tsp) acid dye powder colour.

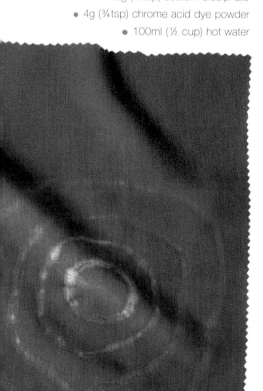

Blue-grey

2hrs   **cold water**

cotton

linen

silk

viscose

This clear, lightfast and washfast colour is produced using cold-water reactive dye. These dyes are also suitable for colour stripping, making them ideal for further painting and printing experiments. Note that extra safety precautions need to be taken when using these dyes in powder form.

1 Wash your fabric in a mild detergent, rinse and dry. Fold the fabric into four and then twist tightly as if wringing out a cloth. Tie strong thread or attach rubber bands down the length of the twisted fabric to secure.

2 Wearing safety clothing, mix the dye powder and hot water in a dye-mixing pot, stirring well to dissolve thoroughly. If it does not dissolve completely, heat or sieve to remove any lumps. For paler or stronger colours, simply vary the amount of dye powder.

3 Fill the dye container with the cold water. Add the dissolved dye and fabric. Over the next 30 minutes, add the salt and the sodium carbonate or sodium bicarbonate. Note that the amount you use depends on how pale or dark a colour you require – less for pale, more for dark. Stir frequently to ensure even distribution of dye over the fabric. Be careful not to pour any powder directly on to the fabric when adding to the container.

4 Leave to dye for another 30 to 90 minutes, depending on the colour required, but continue to stir frequently, making sure the fabric is submerged at all times.

5 Check the colour by rinsing a corner of the fabric and ironing dry. You may need to check a few times to get the strength of colour you want.

6 Remove the fabric and rinse under cold running water. Now remove all the threads and rubber bands to reveal the pattern. Finally, rinse again under cold running water and leave to dry.

You will need

- Safety clothing
- Dye container
- Strong thread or rubber bands
- Glass or metal dye pot for mixing
- Spatula and tongs
- Iron

Ingredients

- 4–6g (¾–1¼tsp) cold-water reactive powder dye
- 100ml (½ cup) hot water
- 10 litres (2 gallons) cold water
- 10–30g (2tsp–1¼oz) household salt
- 5–10g (1–2tsp) washing soda

Alternative colourways You can use more than one colour – for example, adding 4g (¾tsp) of red to 12g (¼oz) of orange will make a warmer orange colour. You can change the colour while you are dyeing by adding more dissolved dye to the dye container, always removing the fabric first. This is useful when you want to make a colour slightly different, for example warmer with red, more acidic with yellow, or duller with green.

12hrs   boil

Blackberry crush

You will need

- Safety clothing
- Dye container
- Glass or metal dye pots for mixing
- Spatula and tongs
- Strainer
- Iron

Ingredients

- 7g (1½tsp) alum
- 7g (1½tsp) cream of tartar
- 150ml (⅔ cup) warm water
- 200g (7oz) blackberries
- 500ml (2 cups) hot water
- Cold water

Although the shoots and leaves of the blackberry plant can be used for dyeing, it is the fruit that yields this attractive plum colour on wool. Although this colour can fade after time, it is an interesting and readily available natural dye, which you can grow, eat and wear!

1 Wash your fabric in a mild detergent, rinse and dry.
2 Wearing safety clothing throughout, next mordant the fabric to improve absorption and to prevent the colour from fading over time, following the instructions on page 24.
3 Place the hot water and blackberries in a dye-mixing pot, bring to the boil and simmer for 20 minutes. Allow to cool and then strain to remove the blackberries.
4 Place the well-rinsed, mordanted fabric in the dye container and fill with cold water to cover the fabric. Add the blackberry liquid and slowly bring to the boil over a 30-minute period. Simmer for 30 minutes, stirring regularly to distribute the dye evenly over the fabric. If necessary, add more water to keep the fabric covered.
5 Check the colour by rinsing a corner of the fabric under cold water and ironing dry. You may need to check a few times to get the strength of colour you want.
6 Allow to cool in the dye container overnight, and then remove and rinse well under plenty of cold running water. Finally, leave to dry.

Oak bark and acorns

7–10 days boil

silk

wool

A ll parts of the oak tree – leaves, acorns, bark and nut-like swellings known as oak galls – can be used to produce stunning shades of brown, grey and ochre. For centuries oak bark was used extensively, with after-mordants, to dye leather and cotton a wonderful golden yellow, but in this recipe it is used on silk in a low concentration to produce a delicate chalky pink. Using acorns instead of bark will produce a similar shade.

1 Wash your fabric in a mild detergent, rinse and dry.
2 Wearing safety clothing throughout, next mordant the fabric to improve absorption and to prevent the colour from fading over time, following the instructions on page 24.
3 Place 500ml (2 cups) of hot water in a glass or metal dye-mixing pot and add the oak bark or acorns. Leave to soak for 7 to 10 days to soften and break down the bark.
4 After soaking, boil the oak bark or acorns for 5 to 10 minutes and then simmer for 30 to 45 minutes. Strain to remove the bark.
5 Place the fabric in the dyeing container and add enough cold water so that the fabric can be moved freely under the water. Add the oak bark or acorn liquid and bring slowly to the boil over a 30-minute period and then simmer for 1 hour, stirring at regular intervals to distribute the dye evenly over the fabric. If necessary, add more water to keep the fabric covered.
6 Check the colour by rinsing a corner of the fabric under cold water and ironing dry. You may need to check a few times to get the strength of colour you want. Allow to cool in the dye container overnight.
7 Remove and rinse well under cold running water and then rinse in warm water with a little mild detergent. Finally, rinse in cold running water and leave to dry.

You will need
- Safety clothing
- Dye container
- Glass or metal dye pots for mixing
- Spatula and tongs
- Iron

Ingredients
- 7g (1½tsp) alum
- 7g (1½tsp) cream of tartar
- 150ml (⅔ cup) warm water
- 200g (7oz) oak bark or acorns
- 500ml (2 cups) hot water

7–10 days   boil

Golden apple bark

You will need

- Safety clothing
- Dye container
- Glass or metal dye pots for mixing
- Spatula and tongs
- Strainer
- Iron

Ingredients

- 7g (1½tsp) alum
- 15g (½oz) cream of tartar
- Cold water
- 150ml (⅔ cup) warm water
- 200g (7oz) of apple bark
- 500ml (2 cups) hot water

The leaves and bark of fruit trees, such as apricot, cherry, peach, pear, and plum, are rich sources of natural dyestuffs. Here, apple bark is used to dye wool a rich shade of golden yellow. Using the appropriate mordant (see page 24), you can adapt this basic recipe to use any fruit tree bark to dye cotton, linen, silk and wool.

1 Wash your fabric in a mild detergent, rinse and dry.
2 Wearing safety clothing throughout, next mordant the fabric to improve absorption and to prevent the colour from fading over time, following the instructions on page 24.
3 Place 500ml (2 cups) of hot water in another glass or metal dye-mixing pot and add the apple bark. Leave to soak for 7 to 10 days to soften and break down the bark.
4 After soaking, boil the bark for 5 to 10 minutes. Simmer for 30 to 45 minutes and then strain to remove the bark.
5 Place the fabric in the dye container and fill with enough cold water so that the fabric can be moved freely under the water. Add the apple bark liquid and bring slowly to the boil over a 30-minute period and then simmer for 1 hour, stirring the fabric at regular intervals to distribute the dye evenly over the fabric. If necessary, add more water to keep the fabric covered.
6 Check the colour by rinsing a corner of the fabric under cold water and ironing dry. You may need to check a few times to get the strength of colour you want. Allow to cool in the dye container overnight.
7 Remove and rinse well under cold running water and then rinse in warm water with a little mild detergent. Finally, rinse in cold running water and leave to dry.

Polyester colouring

1½hrs   95°C (203°F)

Most modern fabrics incorporate polyester fibres, which unfortunately can only be dyed with one type of dye – disperse dye – which needs to be fixed at high temperatures. Try using this recipe to transform plain white polyester net curtains (glass curtains) into a stunning window treatment.

1 Wash the fabric in a mild detergent, rinse and dry.
2 Wearing safety clothing, mix the disperse dye and the boiling water in a dye-mixing pot, stirring well to dissolve.
3 Wearing safety goggles, place 20ml (4tsp) cold water in a dye-mixing pot and add the acetic acid. Always add acid to water, never water to acid. Add this solution to the dye container.
4 Fill the dye container with cold water. Add the dissolved dye, acetic acid, polyester dye carrier, and the fabric, taking care not to pour the ingredients directly onto the fabric. Over the next 15 to 20 minutes, raise the temperature to 90-95°C (194-203°F), just below boiling point. Allow to simmer for 30 to 60 minutes, stirring frequently to distribute the dye evenly over the fabric.
5 Check the colour by rinsing a corner of fabric and ironing dry. You may need to check a few times to get the strength of colour you want.
6 Remove the fabric from the dye container. Rinse under cold running water and then rinse in warm water with a small amount of mild detergent. Finally rinse under cold running water and leave to dry.

You will need
- Safety clothing
- Glass or metal dye pots for mixing
- Spatula and tongs
- Dye container
- Iron

Ingredients
- 2g (⅓tsp) disperse dye powder colour
- 100ml (½ cup) boiling water
- 5ml (1tsp) acid acetic 80% tech
- 20ml (4tsp) cold water
- 1–2g (¼–⅓tsp) polyester dye carrier

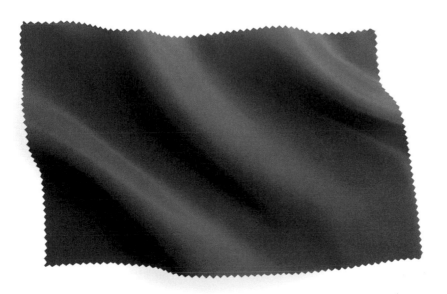

3½ hrs   **boil**

Fustic shibori

This stunning strong yellow shibori fabric is dyed using fustic, obtained from the wood chips of the tree *Chlorophora tinctoria*. Shibori is a resist technique still widely used in Japan today to pattern fabric for kimonos, bags and neckties. The technique involves hand-stitching patterns onto fabric and then pulling the threads tightly before dyeing to create a wide range of resist designs.

You will need
- Safety clothing
- Dye container
- Strong sewing thread
- Glass or metal dye pots for mixing
- Spatula and tongs
- Strainer
- Iron

Ingredients
- 7g (1½tsp) alum
- 7g (1½tsp) cream of tartar
- 150ml (⅔ cup) warm water
- 100g (4oz) fustic chips
- 500ml (2 cups) hot water

1 Wash your fabric in a mild detergent, rinse and dry. Using the strong sewing thread, sew running stitch in even lines across the fabric. Pull the threads tightly to gather the fabric in even pleats, and tie off tightly to prevent any colour penetrating under the stitch lines.

2 Wearing safety clothing throughout, next mordant the fabric to improve absorption and to prevent the colour from fading over time, following the instructions on page 24.

3 Place the fustic chips and hot water in a glass or metal dye-mixing pot and bring to the boil and simmer for 30 to 45 minutes. Allow to cool and then strain to remove the fustic chips.

4 Place the well-rinsed, mordanted fabric in the dyeing container and fill with enough cold water to cover the fabric. Add the fustic liquid and bring slowly to the boil over a 30-minute period and then allow to simmer for 1 hour. Stir at regular intervals to distribute the dye evenly over the fabric. If necessary, add more water to keep the fabric covered.

5 Check the colour by rinsing a corner of fabric under cold water and ironing dry. Remember that wet fabric often dries to a different shade and you may need to check a few times to get the strength of colour you want.

6 Allow to cool in the dye container. Remove and rinse well under cold running water. Now you can remove the sewing threads from the fabric to reveal the pattern. Rinse again in warm water with a little mild detergent. Finally, rinse in cold running water and leave to dry.

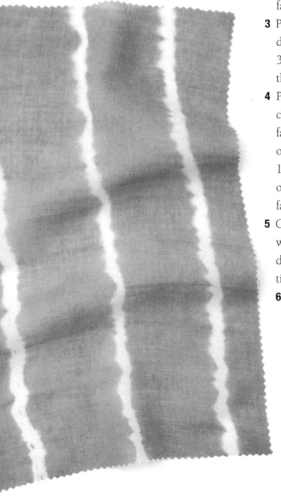

Turmeric squares

1½ hrs   60°C (140°F)

cotton

linen

Although turmeric produces a good orange-yellow colour, it is not as permanent as some other natural or synthetic dyes. It can be dyed without a mordant and at a lower temperature than most natural dyes. Here it is used on cotton in combination with a folded technique that produces an interesting linear pattern.

1 Wash your fabric in a mild detergent, rinse and dry. Concertina-fold the fabric at 7cm (3in) intervals and iron well. Fold this narrow strip of fabric into a small square and iron flat. Tightly wrap the strong thread across both sides to form a cross shape to bind the fabric and form the resist pattern.

2 Wearing safety clothing, mix the hot water and turmeric in a glass or metal dye-mixing pot and bring to the boil and simmer for 30 to 45 minutes. Allow to cool and then strain through the tights (panty hose) to remove any undissolved turmeric powder.

3 Fill the dye container with cold water and add the turmeric liquid and fabric. Start to raise the temperature and increase slowly up to 60°C (140°F). Then simmer for 30 minutes only. Stir the fabric at regular intervals to distribute the dye evenly. If necessary, add more water to keep the fabric covered.

4 Check the colour by rinsing a corner of the fabric under cold water and ironing dry. Remember that wet fabric often dries to a different shade and you may need to check a few times to get the colour you want.

5 When you have the colour you require, remove the fabric and rinse well under cold running water. Now you can remove the thread to reveal the pattern. Rinse in warm water with a little mild detergent and then again in cold running water and leave to dry.

You will need

- Safety clothing
- Strong thread
- Dye container
- Glass or metal dye pot for mixing
- Spatula and tongs
- Pair of old tights (panty hose)
- Iron

Ingredients

- 100g (4oz) turmeric
- 500ml (2 cups) hot water

2hrs **40°-80°C (104°-176°F)**

Retro henna

You will need
- Safety clothing
- Dye container
- Strong thread or rubber bands
- Glass or metal dye pot for mixing
- Spatula and tongs
- Strainer
- Iron

Ingredients
- 100g (4oz) henna
- 500ml (2 cups) hot water

This psychedelic-looking fabric with a feel of the 60s is tie-dyed using henna. Traditionally used in India for body decoration and hair colouring dye, henna will also dye fabrics a mid-brown colour. Obtained from the leaves of the shrub *Lawsonia inermis*, it can dye cellulose fabrics without a mordant. You can also use henna hair dye for a similar effect.

1 Wash your fabric in a mild detergent, rinse and dry. Pick up points on the fabric and bind tightly with strong thread or rubber bands. Place these ties at regular intervals over the fabric to form an even pattern.

2 Wearing safety clothing, mix the hot water and henna in a glass or metal dye-mixing pot. Bring to the boil and then simmer for 30 minutes. Allow to cool and then strain to remove any powder. If using henna hair dye, follow the manufacturer's instructions and mix the henna into a paste.

3 Place the fabric in the dye container and add enough cold water to cover the fabric so that it can be moved freely under the water. Add the henna liquid or paste and bring slowly to the boil over a 30-minute period and then allow to simmer for 1 hour. Stir at regular intervals to distribute the dye evenly over the fabric. If necessary, add more water to keep the fabric covered.

4 Check the colour by rinsing a corner of the fabric under cold water and ironing dry. Remember that wet fabric often dries to a different shade and you may need to check a few times to get the strength of colour you want.

5 Allow to cool in the dye container. Remove and rinse well under cold running water. Remove all the threads or rubber bands and rinse in warm water with a little mild detergent. Finally, rinse in plenty of cold running water and leave to dry.

Tea time

2hrs 30°-80°C (86°-176°F)

We all know the horror of spilling tea or coffee on white fabric and how hard it is to remove the stain. However, this washfast quality of tea and coffee can be used to obtain a good background colour for further decorating techniques. You can also experiment with herbal teas as these provide an additional colour range for your designs.

1 Wash your fabric in a mild detergent, rinse and dry.
2 Wearing safety clothing, place the tea leaves or ground coffee and boiling water in a glass or metal dye-mixing pot, bring back to the boil and simmer for 10 minutes. Allow to cool and then strain to remove the tea or coffee.
3 Place the fabric in the dye container and fill with enough cold water to cover the fabric. Add the tea or coffee liquid and bring slowly to the boil over a 30-minute period and then simmer for 1 hour. Stir at regular intervals to distribute the dye evenly over the fabric. If necessary, add more water to keep the fabric covered at all times.
4 Check the colour by rinsing a corner of the fabric under cold water and ironing dry. Remember that wet fabric often dries to a different shade and you may need to check a few times to get the strength of colour you want.
5 Allow to cool in the dye container and then remove and rinse well under cold running water. Leave to dry.

You will need
- Safety clothing
- Dye container
- Glass or metal dye pots for mixing
- Spatula and tongs
- Strainer
- Iron

Ingredients
- 200g (7oz) dried tea leaves or fresh ground coffee
- 500ml (2 cups) boiling water

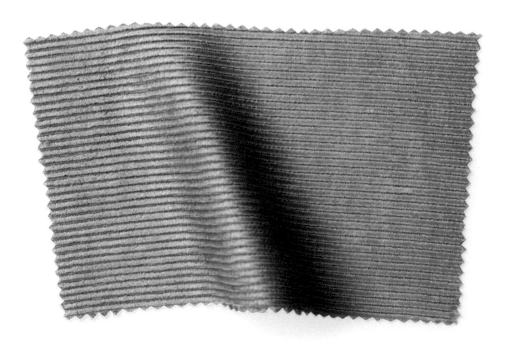

cotton

linen

silk

wool

nylon

viscose

mixed fibres

Multi-purpose dyeing

1hr   40°-80°C
(104°-176°F)

You will need

- Safety clothing
- Dye container
- Glass or metal dye pot for mixing
- Spatula and tongs
- Iron

Ingredients

- 1 small tin of either hot- or cold-water multi-purpose dye
- 500ml (2 cups) boiling water (hot-water dye only)
- 500ml (2 cups) warm water (cold-water dye only)
- 5g (1tsp) household salt (hot-water dye only)
- 20g (¾oz) household salt (cold-water dye only)
- 5g (1tsp) washing soda (cold-water dye only)

Multi-purpose dyes are readily available from most hardware stores and art and craft suppliers. They are one of the easiest dyes to use and are popular for home use as well as small industrial use. Many theatre and ballet companies use these multi-purpose dyes to colour the wide range of fabrics used for costumes. These dyes can be applied to fabric using a dye container, a washing machine or even a microwave oven!

1 Wash your fabric in a mild detergent and rinse well.
2 Wearing safety clothing, place 500ml (2 cups) boiling water or 500ml (2 cups) warm water (depending on the multi-purpose dye you are using) in a glass or metal dye-mixing pot. Add the contents of the dye tin to the pot and stir well to dissolve thoroughly.
3 Place the fabric in a dye container and add enough cold water to allow it to be moved freely under the surface. Add the well-dissolved dye mixture.
4 If you are using hot-water dye, add 5g (1tsp) of household salt and then raise the temperature to the boil. Simmer for 15 to 20 minutes, stirring at regular intervals to distribute the dye evenly and to keep the fabric submerged. If you are using cold-water dye, add 20g (4tsp) of household salt and 5g (1tsp) of washing soda and then leave to soak for 20 to 30 minutes, stirring at regular intervals to distribute the dye evenly over the fabric.
5 When the fabric has dyed, remove and wash in hot water with a small amount of mild detergent. Rinse in cold running water and leave to dry.

Alternative method If using a washing machine, follow the manufacturer's guidelines for hot or cold wash cycles, adding the same ingredients as above. If using a microwave, place the fabric and dissolved dye in a glass or plastic container suitable for microwave use and follow the manufacturer's guidelines for length of time and power settings to cook your fabric in the dye. Rinse well in cold running water and leave to dry. This method will often produce a tie-dyed effect, as it can be hard to get the even distribution of dye needed.

Acid dyes

Acid dyes can produce the most jewel-like colours when used on silk. They can also be used to dye wool and nylon, giving a wide range of rich colours which are very lightfast and washfast.

1 Wash your fabric with a mild detergent to remove any finishes and to wet out the fabric thoroughly so that the dye will take evenly across the whole piece.

2 Fill the dye container with cold water and heat until hand warm.

3 Wearing safety clothing, place 20ml (4tsp) cold water in a dye-mixing pot and add the acetic acid. Always add acid to water, never water to acid. Add this solution to the dye container.

4 In another glass or metal dye-mixing dye pot, dissolve the acid dye powder in the hot water, stirring well to to dissolve any lumps.

5 Add the dissolved dye powder solution to the dye container and stir. Now add the fabric and raise the temperature slowly over a 15-minute period to 80°C (176°F), or just below boiling point, and then simmer for 30 to 60 minutes. Stir at regular intervals to distribute the dye evenly over the fabric. If necessary, add more water to keep the fabric covered.

6 Check the colour by rinsing a corner of the fabric under cold water and ironing dry. Remember that wet fabric often dries to a different shade and you may need to check a few times to get the strength of colour you want. (Note that after the full time in the dye container, the water may be clear. This is called exhausting the dye bath and it means all the dye colour is where it should be – on the fabric!)

7 When you have the required colour, remove the fabric and rinse well in cold running water. Leave to dry.

You will need

- Safety clothing
- Dye container
- Glass or metal dye pots for mixing
- Spatula and tongs
- Iron

Ingredients

- 2g (⅓tsp) acid dye powder colour
- 100ml (½ cup) hot water
- 4ml (¾tsp) acid acetic 80% tech
- 20ml (4tsp) cold water

1hr

80°C
(176°F)

Hot-water reactive dyeing

You will need

- Safety clothing
- Dye container
- Glass or metal dye pot for mixing
- Spatula and tongs
- Iron

Ingredients

- 1–4g (¼–¾tsp) hot-water reactive dye powder colour
- 100ml (½ cup) hot water
- 20–40g (¾–1½oz) household salt

Take extra care when handling reactive powder dyes – always wear a face mask and handle in a well-ventilated area with no draughts.

Synthetic hot-water reactive dyes are extremely light-fast and wash-fast and can be used on a wide range of fabrics, including cotton, linen, viscose and silk. They are ideal for furnishing fabrics, because they will not fade even when used on curtain fabrics destined for a sunny window.

1 Wash the fabric with a mild detergent to remove any surface finishes so that the dye will take evenly across the whole piece.

2 Fill the dye container with enough cold water to cover the fabric so that it can be moved freely under water and heat on an electric or gas ring until the water is hand-warm.

3 Wearing safety clothing, especially a face mask, dissolve 1 to 4g (¼–1tsp) of reactive dye powder in the hot water in a glass or metal dye-mixing pot, stirring well to dissolve any lumps of dye. By varying the amount of dye powder colour, you can obtain paler or stronger colours.

4 Add this dye solution to the dye container and stir. Add the fabric and raise the temperature slowly over a 15-minute period to 80°C (176°F). Add 20 to 40g (1½–3tbsp) salt during this period, taking care not to pour it directly onto your fabric. Increase the amount of salt in line with amount of dye powder colour used. Allow to simmer for 30 to 60 minutes, stirring at regular intervals to distribute the dye evenly over the fabric. If necessary, add more water to keep the fabric covered.

5 Check the colour by rinsing a corner of the fabric under cold water and ironing dry. Remember that wet fabric may dry to a different shade and you may need to check a few times to get the strength of colour you want.

6 When the required colour is achieved, remove the fabric and rinse well in cold running water. Finally, leave to dry.

Comfrey green

1 day   boil

cotton

silk

wool

Widely used over the centuries as a herbal medicine for healing wounds, the fresh leaves of the comfrey plant also have an ability to dye wool, silk and cotton varying shades of green, depending on the mordant used. The dried leaves produce browner shades.

1 Wash your fabric in a mild detergent, rinse and dry.
2 Wearing safety clothing throughout, next mordant the fabric to improve absorption and to prevent the colour from fading over time, following the instructions on page 24.
3 Place 500ml (2 cups) of hot water in another glass or metal dye-mixing pot, add the chopped comfrey leaves, and leave to soak overnight.
4 The following day, bring to the boil and simmer for 30 to 45 minutes. Allow to cool and then strain to remove the leaves.
5 Place the fabric in the dye container and fill with enough cold water to allow the fabric to be moved freely under water and then add the comfrey liquid. Bring slowly to the boil over a 30-minute period and then simmer for 1 hour. Stir at regular intervals to distribute the dye evenly over the fabric. If necessary, add more water to keep the fabric covered.
6 Check the colour by rinsing a corner of the fabric under cold water and ironing dry. Remember that wet fabric may dry to a different shade and you may need to check a few times to get the strength of colour you want.
7 Allow to cool in the dye container and then remove and rinse well under cold running water. Rinse again in warm water with a little mild detergent. Finally, rinse in cold running water and leave to dry.

You will need
- Safety clothing
- Dye container
- Glass or metal dye pots for mixing
- Spatula and tongs
- Strainer
- Iron

Ingredients
- 7g (½tbsp) alum
- 7g (1½tsp) cream of tartar
- 150ml (⅔ cup) warm water
- 200g (7oz) chopped fresh comfrey leaves
- 500ml (2 cups) hot water

1 day   boil

Cutch on cotton

You will need
- Safety clothing
- Dye container
- Approximately ½m (20in) length of wooden pole or plastic pipe
- Rubber bands
- Glass or metal dye pots for mixing
- Spatula and tongs
- Iron

Ingredients
- 50g (1¾oz) alum
- 50g (1¾oz) tannic acid
- 200ml (¾ cup) warm water
- 125g (4½oz) cutch
- 500ml (2 cups) hot water

Cutch, or catech is obtained from the wood of the acacia, areca, or mimosa trees and can be used on cotton, silk or wool fabrics, depending on the mordant used. It produces a good beige–brown colour from its heartwood, and is here used on cotton. In this recipe, a small length of pipe is used to form a physical resist. Pole dyeing can produce a wide variety of patterns depending on the angle and twist used on the fabric and the diameter of the pole. Experiment with this one!

1 Wash your fabric in a mild detergent, rinse and dry.
2 Using a rubber band, attach the fabric to one end of the pole or pipe and wind the fabric tightly along its length. Secure the other end with another rubber band. Now push the fabric back down the pole length, compressing and twisting the fabric as you go. Secure with a rubber band.
3 Wearing safety clothing throughout, next mordant the fabric to improve absorption and to prevent the colour from fading over time, following the instructions on page 24.
4 Place the cutch and hot water in a glass or metal dye-mixing pot. Bring to the boil and simmer for 30 to 45 minutes. Allow to cool and then strain to remove the cutch.
5 Place the well-rinsed, mordanted fabric in the dye container and add enough cold water to cover the fabric. Now add the cutch liquid and the fabric on the pole. Leave to soak overnight. Do not heat. More intense colours can be achieved by soaking the fabric in the dye solution for several days.
6 Check the colour by rinsing a corner of the fabric under cold water and ironing dry. Remember that wet fabric may dry to a different shade and you may need to check a few times to get the strength of colour you want.
7 When you have the colour you require, remove the fabric and rinse well under cold running water. Now you can take off the rubber bands and release the fabric from the pole. Rinse in warm water with a little mild detergent. Finally rinse in cold running water and leave to dry.

Iron rust on silk

2hrs   boil   silk

Iron rust dyes fabric by causing a chemical reaction to take place between the iron rust, the fabric and the air. Although it is often used with other dyeing techniques and additives, in this recipe it is used on its own.

1 Wash the fabric in warm water with a mild detergent to remove any surface finishes so that the dye can take evenly across the whole piece.
2 Wearing safety clothing, fill the dye container with 5 litres (1 gallon) warm water and add the ferrous sulphate. Stir gently to mix.
3 Place your fabric in the dye container and, over a period of 10 to 15 minutes, bring to the boil and then simmer for 5 to 10 minutes. Stir to ensure even distribution of the chemical, making sure the fabric remains submerged at all times.
4 Remove the fabric and spread it out as openly as possible to dry the fabric and allow oxidization to take place.
5 Refill the dye container with 5 litres (1 gallon) warm water and add the sodium carbonate, stirring to dissolve. Place the fabric back in the dye container and leave to soak for 10 to 15 minutes or until the fabric changes from green to a golden rust colour.
6 Rinse in cold running water and then in warm water with a small amount of mild detergent. Finally, rinse in cold water and leave to dry.

You will need
- Safety clothing
- Dye container
- Spatula and tongs

Ingredients
- 2 x 5 litres (1 gallon) warm water
- 500g (18oz) ferrous sulphate
- 10g (2tsp) sodium carbonate

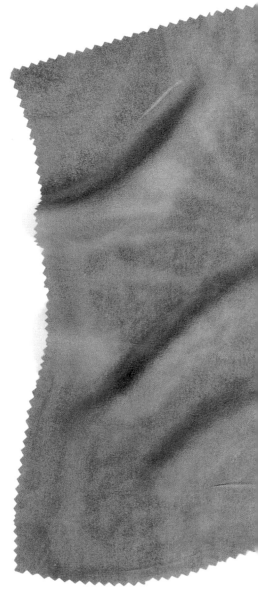

> **Alternative colourway** To achieve an intriguing two-colour effect, try tying peanuts with brown skins onto the fabric with strong thread. Do this at step 1 and then continue with the rest of the process.

3 ½ hrs · boil

Beetle tie-dye

You will need

- Safety clothing
- Dye container
- Keys, washers, coins
- Strong thread or rubber bands
- Glass or metal dye pots for mixing
- Spatula and tongs
- Iron

Ingredients

- 7g (1½tsp) alum
- 7g (1½tsp) cream of tartar
- 150ml (⅔ cup) warm water
- 60g (2¼oz) cochineal
- 150ml (⅔ cup) hot water

Used for centuries to colour wool and silk, the dye produced from cochineal beetles is one of the oldest natural dyes. Collected in South America, the dried beetle produces a vivid, lightfast red on wool fabrics. In this recipe, an interesting abstract pattern is created by tying found objects such as keys, washers and coins into the fabric before dyeing with the cochineal.

1 Wash your fabric in a mild detergent, rinse and dry. Now sew or tie the keys, washers and coins into your fabric to form a pattern using the strong thread or rubber bands.

2 Wearing safety clothing throughout, next mordant the fabric to improve absorption and to prevent the colour from fading over time, following the instructions on page 24.

3 Pour the hot water into a glass or metal dye-mixing pot and add the cochineal. Bring to the boil and simmer for 30 to 45 minutes. Allow to cool and then strain the liquid to remove the cochineal.

4 Fill the dye container with enough cold water so that the fabric can be moved around easily under water and add the cochineal liquid and fabric. Bring slowly to the boil over a period of 30 minutes. Allow to simmer for 1 hour, stirring at regular intervals to ensure even distribution of the dye. If necessary, add more water to keep the fabric covered.

5 Check the colour by rinsing a piece of the fabric under cold water and ironing dry. Wet fabric may dry to a different shade and you may need to check a few times before you get the strength of colour required.

6 Allow the dye container to cool and then remove the fabric and rinse well under cold running water. Now remove the tied objects from the fabric and rinse again in warm water with a little mild detergent. Finally, rinse again in cold running water and leave to dry.

Alternative colourway Note that the cochineal dye liquid can be used several times, although each time it is used, it will produce a lighter, pinker shade. If a more intense red is required, repeat step 3 and add to the remaining liquid

Colour direct

1hr   30°-80°C
(86°-176°F)

cotton

linen

viscose

Direct dyes are some of the simplest synthetic hot-water dyes to use, because it is easy to control the depth and shade of colour while the fabric is in the dye container. As soon as your fabric reaches a shade that you like, simply remove it from the dye container and rinse.

1 Wash the fabric in warm water with a mild detergent to remove any surface finishes so that the dye will take evenly across the whole piece.

2 Fill the dye container with enough cold water to cover the fabric so it can be moved freely under the water and heat on an electric or gas ring until hand-warm.

3 Wearing safety clothing, dissolve the direct dye powder in the hot water in a glass or metal dye-mixing pot, stirring well to dissolve any lumps of dye. (To deepen the shade of colour, add more dye powder colour in increments of ½–1g (⅟₁₆–¼tsp.)

4 Add this dye solution to the dye container and stir. Now add the fabric and raise the temperature slowly over a 15-minute period to 80°C (176°F), or just below boiling point. Add the salt during this period, taking care not to pour it directly onto the fabric. Allow to simmer for 30 to 60 minutes, stirring at regular intervals to distribute the dye evenly over the fabric. If necessary, add more water to keep the fabric covered.

5 Check the colour by rinsing a corner of the fabric under cold water and ironing dry. Remember that wet fabric may dry to a different shade and you may need to check a few times to get the strength of colour you want.

6 When the required colour is achieved, remove the fabric and rinse well in plenty of cold running water. Finally, leave to dry.

You will need

- Safety clothing
- Dye container
- Glass or metal dye pot for mixing
- Spatula and tongs
- Iron

Ingredients

- 2g (⅓tsp) direct dye powder colour
- 100ml (½ cup) hot water
- 20g (¾oz) household salt

1 day   40°-80°C
               (104°-176°F)

You will need

- Safety clothing
- Dye container
- Glass or metal dye
  pots for mixing
- Spatula and tongs
- Old tights (pantyhose)
- Iron

Ingredients

- 7g (1½tsp) alum
- 7g (1½tsp) cream of tartar
- 150ml (⅔ cup) warm water
- 200g (7oz) dried
  safflower flowers
- 500ml (2 cups) hot water
- 5g (1tsp) potassium carbonate

Safflower two-in-one

Safflower is a most unusual natural dye in that the same dried flowers can be used twice over to produce two primary colours. The first colour, yellow, must be extracted before the second colour, red, can be obtained. The yellow colour can be used with cotton, linen, silk and wool, whilst the red colour will only fix to cotton, linen and silk. Note that you should always wear rubber gloves when using safflower, because it can stain your skin.

To dye wool yellow

1 Wash your fabric in a mild detergent, rinse and dry.
2 Wearing safety clothing throughout, next you need to mordant the fabric, following the instructions on page 24.
3 Place the hot water and dried safflower flowers in a glass or metal dye-mixing pot, bring to the boil and simmer for 30 to 45 minutes. Allow to cool and then strain the liquid through the tights (pantyhose) to remove the flowers. Save the flowers if you want to dye cotton red (see below).
4 Place your well-rinsed, mordanted fabric in the dye container and add enough cold water to cover it. Add the safflower liquid and bring slowly to the boil over a 30-minute period and then simmer for 1 hour. Stir the fabric at regular intervals distribute the dye evenly. If necessary, add more water to keep the fabric covered.
5 Check the colour by rinsing a corner of the fabric under cold water and ironing dry. Remember that wet fabric often dries to a different shade and you may need to check a few times to get the strength of colour you want.
6 Allow to cool in the dye container. Remove and rinse well under cold running water. and then rinse again in warm water with a little mild detergent. Finally, rinse in cold running water and leave to dry.

To dye cotton red

1 Wash your fabric in a mild detergent, rinse and dry.
2 Fill the dye container with cold water and add the potassium carbonate and the old tights (pantyhose) containing the dried flowers from stage 3 above. Leave to stand for 60 to 90 minutes.
3 Remove the safflowers, add the fabric and leave to dye overnight. Do not heat the dye container.
4 The following day, remove the fabric and rinse well under cold water. Leave to dry thoroughly.

Heather button resist

3½ hrs   30°-80°C
(86°-176°F)

Most heathers will make a yellow dye, but it is the flowering tips of *Calluna vulgaris* that provide the best dyestuff. This interesting resist pattern is created from the stitches used to sew a variety of buttons in different shapes and sizes to the fabric.

1 Wash your fabric in a mild detergent, rinse and dry. Sew the buttons randomly on the fabric with a strong thread, pulling the stitches tightly to form the resist pattern.
2 Wearing safety clothing throughout, next mordant the fabric to improve absorption and to prevent the colour from fading over time, following the instructions on page 24.
3 In a glass or metal dye-mixing pot, add 500ml (2 cups) of hot water and 100g (½ cup) of dried heather. Bring to the boil and simmer for 45 minutes. Allow to cool and then strain to remove the heather.
4 Place the fabric in the dye container and add enough cold water to cover the fabric. Add the heather liquid and bring slowly to the boil over a 30-minute period and then simmer for 1 hour. Stir at regular intervals to distribute the dye evenly over the fabric. If necessary, add more water to keep the fabric covered.
5 Check the colour by rinsing a corner of the fabric under cold water and ironing dry. Remember that wet fabric often dries to a different shade and you may need to check a few times to get the strength of colour you want.
6 Allow to cool in the dye container. Remove and rinse well under cold running water and then rinse again in warm water with a little mild detergent. Now you can remove all the buttons to reveal the pattern. Finally, rinse again in cold running water and allow to dry thoroughly.

> **Alternative colourways** A range of shades from deep rust through green to yellow can be obtained by using the flowers, plant tops or dried heather. As there are many different types of heather, there are a wide range of colour possibilities so make sure you test the colour each time.

You will need
- Safety clothing
- Dye container
- Various buttons and strong thread
- Glass or metal dye pots for mixing
- Spatula and tongs
- Strainer
- Iron

Ingredients
- 7g (1½ tsp) alum
- 7g (1½ tsp) cream of tartar
- 150ml (⅔ cup) warm water
- 100g (4oz) dried heather
- 500ml (2 cups) hot water

2 days　　　　**boil**

Hollyhock purple

You will need

- Safety clothing
- Dye container
- Glass or metal dye pots for mixing
- Spatula and tongs
- Strainer
- Iron

Ingredients

- 7g (1½tsp) alum
- 7g (1½tsp) cream of tartar
- 150ml (⅔ cup) warm water
- Cold water
- 200g (7oz) fresh or dried hollyhock flowers
- 500ml (2 cups) hot water

Hollyhocks are easy to grow in your own garden to use as a natural dye – you can either pick the flowers and use them fresh or dry them to use later. Wool – luxurious cashmere in particular – absorbs the intense colours of hollyhocks well, producing rich shades of mauve, maroon and purple.

1 Wash your fabric in a mild detergent, rinse and dry.
2 Wearing safety clothing throughout, next mordant the fabric to improve absorption and to prevent the colour from fading over time, following the instructions on page 24.
3 Place 500ml (2 cups) of hot water in a glass or metal dye-mixing pot. Add the hollyhock flowers, bring to the boil and simmer for 30–45 minutes.
4 Leave to soak and cool overnight and then strain the liquid to remove the flowers.
5 Place the fabric in the dye container and add enough cold water to cover the fabric so that it can be moved freely under the water. Add the hollyhock liquid and bring slowly to the boil over a 30-minute period. Simmer for 1 hour, stirring at regular intervals to distribute the dye evenly over the fabric. If necessary, add more water to keep the fabric covered. Allow to cool in the dye container overnight.
6 Remove and rinse well under cold running water and then rinse in warm water with a little mild detergent. Finally, rinse in cold running water and leave to dry.

Logwood maroon

2½ hrs   boil

Used as a dyestuff since the sixteenth century, logwood produces a range of rich purple colours. When using logwood to dye wool, it is worth trying out the different types of mordant outlined on page 24 to see the different shades of purple – from grey violet through maroon to deep blueish purple – that can be obtained.

1 Wash your fabric in a mild detergent, rinse and dry.
2 Wearing safety clothing throughout, next mordant the fabric to improve absorption and to prevent the colour from fading over time, following the instructions on page 24.
3 Place 500ml (2 cups) of hot water in another glass or metal dye-mixing pot and add the dried logwood chips. Bring to the boil and simmer for 20 to 30 minutes. Allow to cool and then strain to remove the chips.
4 Place the fabric in the dye container and add enough cold water to cover the fabric so that it can be moved freely under the water. Add the logwood liquid and bring slowly to the boil over a 30-minute period. Simmer for 30 minutes, stirring at regular intervals to distribute the dye evenly over the fabric. If necessary, add more water to keep the fabric covered.
5 Check the colour by rinsing a corner of the fabric under cold water and ironing dry. Remember that wet fabric may dry to a different shade and you may need to check a few times to get the strength of colour you want.
6 Allow to cool in the dye container and then rinse well under cold running water. Rinse again in warm water with a little mild detergent. Finally, rinse in cold running water and leave to dry.

You will need
- Safety clothing
- Dye container
- Glass or metal dye pots for mixing
- Spatula and tongs
- Strainer
- Iron

Ingredients
- 7g (1½tsp) alum
- 7g (1½tsp) cream of tartar
- 150ml (⅔ cup) warm water
- 100g (4oz) dried logwood chips
- Cold water
- 500ml (2 cups) hot water

1½hrs   80°C (176°F)

Cross-dyed velvet

You will need

- Safety clothing
- Dye container
- Glass or metal dye pots for mixing
- Spatula and tongs
- Iron

Ingredients

- 1–2g (¼–⅓tsp) acid dye powder colour
- 4g (¾tsp) direct dye powder colour
- 2 x 100ml (½ cup) hot water
- 4ml (¾tsp) acid acetic 80% tech
- 20ml (4tsp) cold water
- 20-40g (¾–1½oz) household salt

This attractive devoré velvet design is achieved by cross-dyeing with acid dyes (which colour the silk) and direct dyes (which colour the viscose). The two-colour technique is extremely effective in emphasizing the contrast between the pile of the velvet and the soft silk-chiffon background.

1 Wash the fabric in a mild detergent, rinse and dry.

2 Wearing safety clothing, mix the acid dye powder colour and the hot water together in a glass or metal dye-mixing pot, stirring well to dissolve thoroughly. By varying the amount of dye powder, you can obtain paler or stronger colours. In another dye-mixing pot, mix the direct dye with the hot water, stirring well to dissolve thoroughly.

3 Wearing safety goggles, place 20ml (4tsp) cold water in a dye-mixing pot and add the acetic acid. Always add acid to water, never water to acid.

4 Fill the dye container with enough cold water to cover the fabric so that it can be moved easily under the water. Add both the dissolved dye powder colours, the dissolved acetic acid, the salt, and the fabric. Take care not to pour the ingredients directly onto the fabric when adding to the container. Over the next 20 to 30 minutes, raise the temperature to 80°C (176°F), or just below boiling point. Simmer for 30 to 60 minutes, stirring frequently to distribute the dye evenly.

5 Check the colour by rinsing a corner of the fabric and ironing dry. Remember that wet fabric may dry to a different shade and you may need to check a few times to get the colour you want.

6 Remove the fabric from the dye container and rinse under cold running water and leave to dry. The acid dye will have coloured the silk and the direct dye will have coloured the viscose.

> **Alternative method** This technique can also be used on other two-fibre fabrics including devoré silk satin. It relies on the dye's affinity to its own fabric type – acid dye for silk, direct dye for viscose. Note that only some of the dyes in the acid and direct range work in this way, so always test first. I have found that the higher the wash-fastness rating in the opposite fabric type – 4–5 rating of acid dye on cotton and 4–5 rating of direct dye on silk – the more likely it is to cross-dye. You can also use just the acid dye and acetic acid in this recipe to achieve a dark silk background with a pale velvet pile.

Manganese bronze

1hr 20°C (66°F) silk

Y ou can obtain an intense brown colour on silk by dyeing fabric in manganese chloride, also known as "manganese bronze". Because it is hard to achieve an even, flat colour, this dyestuff is commonly used with a resist technique, or on heavily textured fabrics such as the silk used here.

1 Wash the fabric with a mild detergent to remove any surface finishes so that the dye can take evenly across the whole piece. Leave to dry.

2 Wearing safety clothing, fill the dye container with 5 litres (1 gallon) of warm water and add the manganese chloride, stirring thoroughly to mix.

3 Place the fabric in the dye container and, keeping it submerged at all times, leave for 5 to 10 minutes to allow full colour absorption from the manganese chloride. Remove the fabric and leave to dry, spreading the fabric out as openly as possible.

4 Taking extreme care and wearing rubber gloves, apron and safety goggles, in a glass dye-mixing pot, dissolve the sodium hydroxide solution in 100ml (½ cup) of cold water. Always add sodium hydroxide to water, never water to sodium hydroxide.

5 Refill the dye container with 5 litres (1 gallon) of warm water and add the dissolved sodium hydroxide solution, stirring gently. Still wearing all safety clothing, wash the fabric in this solution for a few minutes to fix the manganese onto the fabric.

6 In a glass dye-mixing pot, dissolve the acetic acid in 10ml (2tsp) of cold water. Always add acid to water, never water to acid.

7 Wash the fabric in warm water containing the dissolved acetic acid solution for 2 to 3 minutes. This will restore the fabric's natural balance. Rinse in cold running water and then wash again in warm water with a small amount of mild detergent. Finally, rinse in plenty of cold running water and leave to dry.

You will need
- Safety clothing
- Strong thread or rubber bands
- Gravel
- Dye container
- Glass dye pots for mixing
- Spatula and tongs
- Iron

Ingredients
- 2 x 5 litres (1 gallon) warm water
- 500g (18oz) manganese chloride
- 2ml (½tsp) sodium hydroxide solution 72°TW
- 100ml (½ cup) cold water
- 2ml (½tsp) acid acetic 80% tech
- 10ml (2tsp) cold water

1hr   80°C
(176°F)

One-colour shading

You will need

- Safety clothing
- Rubber band
- Plastic bag
- Dye container
- Glass or metal dye pots for mixing
- Spatula and tongs
- Iron

Ingredients

- 4ml (¾tsp) acid acetic 80% tech
- 20ml (4tsp) cold water
- 0.5g (⅛tsp) acid dye powder colour
- 1g (¼tsp) acid dye powder colour
- 2g (⅓tsp) acid dye powder colour
- 3 x 100ml (½ cup) hot water

In India, silk saris are sometimes dyed in a gradation of rich colours using locally produced vegetable dyes such as ochre and indigo. This recipe uses three different strengths of blue acid dye to create the effect of an intense blue-black gradually fading away to the palest aquamarine, and finally white, but it works equally well with other colourways.

1 Wash the fabric with a mild detergent to remove any finishes so that the dye will take evenly across the whole piece. Leave to dry. Place the end of the fabric that you require to stay white in a clean plastic bag and tie with a rubber band to prevent any dye contamination.

2 Fill the dye container with enough cold water so that the fabric can be moved around freely under the water and heat on an electric or gas ring until hand-warm.

3 Wearing safety clothing, place 20ml (4tsp) of cold water in a glass or metal dye-mixing pot and add the acetic acid. Always add acid to water, never water to acid. Add this solution to the dye container.

4 Now make up your 3 shades of colour. In 3 separate glass or metal dye-mixing pots, dissolve the 3 amounts of acid dye powder, each in 100ml (½ cup) of hot water, stirring well to dissolve any lumps of dye.

5 Add a small amount of the weakest colour solution to the dye container and immerse the fabric, taking care to

ensure the plastic bag does not go into the dye container.

6 Raise the temperature slowly over the next 20 to 30 minutes to 80°C (176°F), or just below boiling point, adding more of the weakest colour solution and raising the fabric further out of the dye container at the same time. Add the other two colour solutions in the same way while the temperature is still rising, taking care not to scald yourself. Ensure that you raise the fabric in an even manner to achieve a clean, even gradation.

7 Leave the last remaining piece of fabric that requires the darkest colour in the dye container to simmer for 10 to 15 minutes.

8 When finished, rinse in cold running water and then remove the rubber band and plastic bag. Finally, rinse in cold running water and leave to dry.

> **Alternative method** Once you have got used to raising the fabric as you raise the temperature, you can try doing a gradation dye using just one strong strength of dye solution, raising the fabric and using your eye to judge the evenness of the colour gradation.

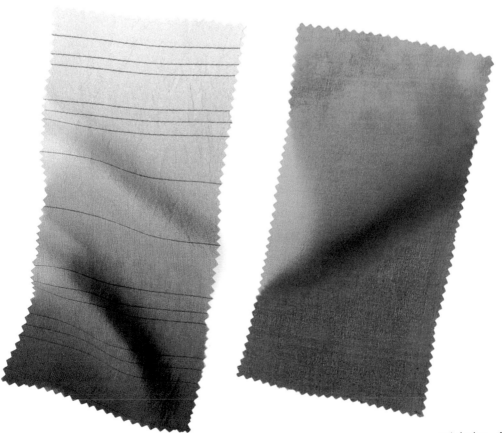

3 ½ hrs   boil

Chamomile yellow

You will need

- Safety clothing
- Dye container
- Glass or metal dye pots for mixing
- Spatula and tongs
- Strainer
- Iron

Ingredients

- 7g (1½ tsp) alum
- 15g (½ oz) cream of tartar
- 150ml (⅔ cup) warm water
- 200g (7oz) of dried chamomile flowers
- 500ml (2 cups) hot water

The dried yellow flowers of the chamomile plant *Anthemis tinctoria* have been used as a dyestuff for several centuries and are known as "dyer's chamomile". The flowers produce a beautiful yellow colour on woollen fabrics.

1 Wash your fabric in a mild detergent, rinse and dry.
2 Wearing safety clothing throughout, next mordant the fabric to improve absorption and to prevent the colour from fading over time, following the instructions on page 24.
3 Place the dried chamomile and hot water in a glass or metal mixing dye pot and bring to the boil and simmer for 30 to 45 minutes. Allow to cool and then strain to remove the flowers.
4 Place the well-rinsed, mordanted fabric in the dyeing container and fill with enough cold water so that it can be moved freely under the water. Add the chamomile liquid and bring slowly to the boil over a 30-minute period and then simmer for 1 hour. Stir the fabric at regular intervals to distribute the dye evenly over the fabric. If necessary, add more water to keep the fabric covered.
5 Check the colour by rinsing a corner of the fabric under cold water and ironing dry. Remember that wet fabric looks a totally different colour when dry, and you may need to check a few times to get the strength of colour you want.
6 Allow to cool in the dye container. Remove the fabric and rinse well under cold running water and then rinse again in warm water with a little mild detergent. Finally rinse in cold running water and leave to dry.

Weld accordion

3½ hrs   80°C (176°F)

silk

wool

W eld, *Reseda luteda* or "dyer's rocket", is one of the most economical of natural dyes, with all but the root being used to produce a strong and lightfast yellow. By using this folding and tying method to pattern the fabric, you can create simple yet elegant graphic designs.

1 Wash your fabric in a mild detergent, rinse and dry. Fold the fabric in accordion-pleats about 5cm (2in) wide. Tie securely with strong thread or rubber bands at regular intervals of 5cm (2in) to form a dye resist.

2 Wearing safety clothing throughout, next mordant the fabric to improve absorption and to prevent the colour from fading over time, following the instructions on page 24.

3 In a glass or metal dye-mixing pot, add the 500ml (2 cups) of hot water to the weld. Raise the temperature to 80°C (176°F), or just below boiling point, and then simmer for 30 to 45 minutes. Be careful not to boil as this can affect the colour. Allow to cool and then strain to remove the weld.

4 Place the well-rinsed, mordanted fabric in the dye container and refill with enough cold water so that the fabric can be moved freely under the water. Add the weld liquid and slowly bring to the boil over a 30-minute period and then simmer for 1 hour. Stir at regular intervals to distribute the dye evenly over the fabric. If necessary, add more water to keep the fabric covered.

5 Check the colour by rinsing a corner of the fabric under cold water and ironing dry. Remember that wet fabric may dry to a different shade and you may need to check a few times to get the strength of colour you want.

6 Allow to cool in the dye container. Remove and rinse well under cold running water and then rinse again in warm water with a little mild detergent. Now you can remove all the threads or rubber bands to release the fabric and reveal your pattern. Rinse again in cold running water and leave to dry.

You will need
- Dye container
- Strong sewing thread or rubber bands
- Glass or metal dye pots for mixing
- Spatula and tongs
- Strainer
- Iron

Ingredients
- 7g (1½ tsp) alum
- 7g (1½ tsp) cream of tartar
- 150ml (⅔ cup) warm water
- 150g (5½ oz) weld
- 500ml (2 cups) hot water

cotton

linen

silk

wool

viscose

mixed fibres

5-6 days

20°C
(68°F)

Marbling

You will need

- Safety clothing
- Marbling tray
- Large glass or plastic dye pot for mixing
- Spatula and tongs
- Hand-held electric mixer or blender
- Iron
- Dropper
- Clean newsprint
- Comb, knitting needle or fork

Ingredients

- 10g (2tsp) carrageenan
- 5g (1tsp) washing soda
- 1 litre (4 cups) warm water
- Small amounts opaque pure pigment colour

Marbling is usually associated with paper, but fabulous effects can also be achieved on small pieces of fabric. The size of fabric is limited by the size of your marbling tray – photographic or cat-litter trays are ideal, so marbling your living-room curtains might be a little tricky! This recipe shows you how to mix your own marbling colours and medium, but kits containing all the ingredients you need are also available.

1 Wash the fabric with a mild detergent to remove any surface finishes and to thoroughly wet the fabric so that the dye can take evenly across the whole piece.

2 Wearing safety clothing, mix the carrageenan, washing soda and warm water in a large glass or plastic dye-mixing pot using a hand-held mixer or blender. Pour this mixture into the marbling tray.

3 Repeat stage 2 until the mixture in the marbling tray is approximately 5cm (2in) deep. Leave to stand for 12 hours or overnight.

4 Next mordant the fabric to improve absorption and help the marbling to fix to the fibres. Mordant according to the type of fabric, following the instructions on page 24.

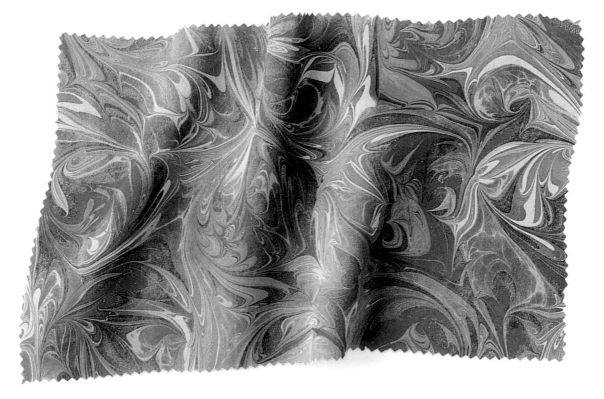

5 Before using the marbling bath, carefully skim the surface of the solution with clean newsprint to remove any impurities.

6 Using a dropper, drop a small amount of each opaque pure pigment colour onto the surface of the solution. Each drop will form a 4 to 6cm (1½-2½ in) spread of colour, or "stone", on the surface of the solution. When you have enough "stones", use a comb, knitting needle or fork to move or drag each one across the surface to form a marble effect.

7 When you have a pattern you like, place your fabric carefully on the surface of the patterned solution, starting at one end and laying the fabric carefully down the length of the tray so as not to disturb the pattern underneath. Leave to rest on the surface for 45 to 60 seconds.

8 Remove the fabric, keeping the design intact, by carefully lifting up both short sides of the fabric at the same time, holding it as flat as possible so as not to damage the design. Keeping the fabric as flat as possible, rinse under cold running water and leave to dry flat. Leave flat for 4 to 5 days to cure the design. Press the back of the fabric with a hot iron for 2 to 3 minutes.

Alternative colourway There are hundreds of formal marbling patterns, details of which can be found in the many books available on marbling. However, do try experimenting with different objects and colour combinations to produce interesting effects of your own. When dragging the pattern, always take care not to overwork the "stones" in the tray by moving them too many times, otherwise they will lose their clarity of colour.

1hr   boil

Wire tie-dye

You will need

- Safety clothing
- Dye container
- Various thicknesses of wire
- Glass dye pots for mixing
- Spatula and tongs

Ingredients

- 500g (18oz) ferrous sulphate
- 500g (18oz) tannic acid powder
- 5 litres (1 gallon) warm water

In this recipe, fine silk was first tied with various thicknesses of wire to make a resist pattern and then dyed with a mixture of tannic acid and ferrous salt. Although these chemicals are not usually used as fabric dyes, the combination of these two chemicals in a dye container results in a wonderful light-fast colour.

1 Wash the fabric with a mild detergent to remove any finishes so that the dye will take evenly across the whole piece. Leave to dry. Using the various thicknesses of wire, tie the fabric tightly in sections to form a resist pattern.

2 Wearing safety clothing, fill the dye container with the warm water and the ferrous sulphate, stirring gently to mix. Add the fabric and raise the temperature to the boil over a period of 10 to 15 minutes. Allow to simmer for 5 to 10 minutes, stirring frequently to ensure even distribution of the chemical.

3 Using the tongs, carefully remove the fabric and add the tannic acid powder to the dye container and stir to mix.

4 Place the fabric back in the dye container and leave to soak for 10 to 15 minutes, stirring frequently to ensure even distribution of the chemical.

5 Remove the fabric and rinse under cold running water. Now untie the wire and rinse the fabric in warm water with a small amount of mild detergent. Finally, rinse again in cold water and leave to dry.

Dyer's alkanet

3½ hrs   boil

cotton

linen

silk

wool

Dyer's alkanet, which comes from the chopped root of the borage-related plant *Alkanna tinctoria*, has been used for centuries as a dyestuff. Depending on the type of fabric and mordant used with the alkanet, a colour range from grey through to pale lilac can be obtained. While it is not a very permanent dye, it has the ability to fade to very pleasing shades of the original colour obtained.

1 Wash your fabric in a mild detergent, rinse and dry.
2 Wearing safety clothing throughout, next mordant the fabric to improve absorption and to prevent the colour from fading over time, following the instructions on page 24.
3 Place the dyer's alkanet in a metal dye-mixing pot and add the methylated spirits, mixing together well. Add the hot water and bring to the boil. Simmer for 45 minutes. Allow to cool and then strain the liquid to remove the alkanet.
4 Place the fabric in the dye container and add enough cold water so that the fabric can be moved freely under the water. Add the alkanet liquid and bring slowly to the boil over a 30-minute period and then simmer for 1 hour. Stir at regular intervals to distribute the dye evenly over the fabric. If necessary, add more water to keep the fabric covered.
5 Check the colour by rinsing a corner of the fabric under cold water and ironing dry. Remember that wet fabric may dry to a different shade and you may need to check a few times to get the strength of colour you want.
6 Allow to cool in the dye container. Remove and rinse well under cold running water and then rinse again in warm water with a little mild detergent. Finally, rinse again in cold running water and allow to dry thoroughly.

You will need
- Safety clothing
- Dye container
- Glass or metal dye pots for mixing
- Spatula and tongs
- Strainer
- Iron

Ingredients
- 7g (1½ tsp) alum
- 75g (2¾ oz) cream of tartar
- 150ml (⅔ cup) warm water
- 100g (4oz) dyer's alkanet
- 50ml (¼ cup) methylated spirits
- 500ml (2 cups) hot water

Alternative colourway A less intense colour is obtained if you leave out the methylated spirits. You can also soak the dyer's alkanet in methylated spirits for 20 to 30 minutes before adding the hot water, to increase the lilac shading in the final colouring, but you will need to add enough methylated spirits to cover the dye root.

painting

In this section, dyes or chemical pastes are applied by brush or by roller to create highly patterned fabrics. All the recipes in this section will paint one square metre (nine square feet) of fabric.

1 hr   3–5 mins

Silver leaf

The most opulent and extravagant of fabrics can be created by using gold or silver pigment dyes. To make the look more varied and subtle, this recipe shows you how to tone down the gold and silver colours by adding other pigment colours and by using pearlized pigment dyes on light-coloured fabric. You can also use this recipe in combination with stencilling and screen-printing techniques.

You will need
- Safety clothing
- Pins or tape
- Paintbrushes
- Glass or plastic dye pots with lids for mixing and storing
- Spatula
- Iron

Ingredients
- 200g (7oz) metallic pigment binder
- 60g (2¼oz) gold, silver or pearlized powder pigment colour
- 60g (2¼oz) pure pigment colour (optional)

Handle the metallic pigments with extra care – mix in a well-ventilated area with no draughts and always wear a mask when stirring

1 Press the fabric well and, using pins or tape, attach it to your printing table (see page 30).

2 Wearing full safety clothing, place the metallic pigment binder in a glass or plastic dye-mixing pot. Carefully fold the metallic pigment powder colour into the binder and then stir to mix thoroughly.

3 Using the paste mixed in step 2, paint the design onto the fabric. For best results, on a dark background, first paint your design in plain pure pigment colour and then, when dry, paint over it again with metallic pigment colour. As it is hard to paint precisely on top of a design, the edges and areas left showing underneath the metallic colour help create a strong three-dimensional image.

4 Allow to dry completely. To speed up the drying process, you can use a fan heater or hair dryer.

5 When the design is completed and dry, iron on the back of the fabric with a hot iron for 3 to 5 minutes, pressing firmly to fix the pattern into the fabric.

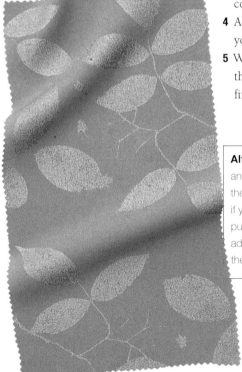

Alternative colourway There are several ways to make gold and silver pigment dyes more subtle. For a hint of bronze, add the tiniest amount of brown pure pigment colour to the gold, or if you want a gunmetal colour, add the tiniest amount of black pure pigment colour to silver. To produce a two-tone effect, add a tiny amount of a complementary pure pigment colour to the pearlized pigment colour.

Gingko silk

2 hrs 15 mins

cotton

silk

viscose

linen

Simple outlines of gingko leaves are painted onto silk in this recipe to create a beautiful, harmonious design. The reactive dye powder colours used here are a very versatile range of dyes suitable for several recipes throughout this book.

1 Press fabric well and, using pins or tape, attach it to your printing table (see page 30).
2 Wearing safety clothing, make the thickening binder into a paste by mixing the sodium alginate thickener with 250ml (1 cup) of warm water in a glass or plastic dye-mixing pot using an electric hand mixer or blender.
3 Place 125ml (½ cup) of hot water in a glass or metal dye-mixing pot and add 5 to 10g (1–2tsp) reactive dye powder colour, depending on the strength of colour required. Stir well to dissolve all the powder. While still hot, add the urea, stirring well.
4 Add the reactive dye and urea solution to the thickening paste in the glass or plastic dye-mixing pot and mix until smooth. Leave to cool.
5 Add the sodium bicarbonate and wetting out agent to this mixture and stir thoroughly until a smooth paste is formed.
6 Do this for each of the colours required. Kept in airtight containers, these dye paste colours will last several weeks. When they become runny in consistency, they can no longer be used.
7 Using this dye mixture, paint your design onto the fabric, allowing each colour to dry fully before applying the next.
8 Now fix the dyes onto the fabric by steaming for 15 minutes, following the instructions on page 25 .
9 After steaming, wash off carefully to avoid any unfixed dye staining undecorated areas. Wash in cold water and then warm water with a small amount of mild detergent. Finally, rinse in cold running water and leave to dry.

Alternative colourway Not all reactive acid dye powder colours are suitable for this paste recipe, so be sure to do a test sample before starting a large piece of work. In general, P reactive dye colours are suitable for this recipe.

You will need
- Safety clothing
- Pins and masking tape
- Thick paintbrush
- Glass or plastic dye pots with lids for mixing and storing
- Electric hand mixer or blender
- Glass or metal dye pots for mixing
- Spatula
- Small steamer

Ingredients
- 25g (1oz) sodium alginate thickener
- 250ml (1 cup) warm water
- 5–10g (1–2 tsp) reactive dye powder colour
- 125ml (½ cup) hot water
- 60g (2¼oz) urea
- 8g (1¾ tsp) sodium bicarbonate
- 5ml (1tsp) wetting out agent

cotton

linen

silk

wool

viscose

mixed fibres

2hrs   cold water

Abstract wax

- Safety clothing
- Wooden frame to fit your fabric
- Drawing pins (thumbtacks)
- Paintbrushes
- Iron

Ingredients
- 50ml (¼ cup) ceramic wax resist

This stunning fabric was patterned using a ready-to-use cold liquid ceramic wax resist. Depending on the method you use to apply the wax, you can produce a variety of effects, ranging from solid resisted areas to fabulous speckled effects. This wax resist technique works best on finer fabrics.

1 Pin out your fabric on an open wooden frame, such as an old picture frame or artists' stretcher bars. Using drawing pins (thumbtacks), attach the fabric to the frame. It's easiest to start in the middle of the longest side and attach the fabric to the frame with 3 pins at intervals of 5cm (2in). Go to the other longest side and repeat this process, pulling the fabric taut across the frame. Do the same to the two shorter sides, and then continue to pin and stretch all the way around your frame, working from alternate sides each time.

2 Wearing safety clothing, paint your design onto the fabric using the liquid wax. Clean your brushes in hot water after use. Allow the wax to dry thoroughly before dyeing.

3 To colour your fabric, follow the recipe for indigo on page 72, or blue-grey on page 79, or cold-water multi-purpose dyeing on page 88. Immerse the fabric in the dye bath, keeping it as open as possible.

4 To build up a multi-coloured fabric, you can either add or take away wax with hot water, protecting the coloured areas with wax to make a more interesting design. Each different colour will need to be applied using one of the cold-water dye methods listed in step 3.

5 If you need to remove only a small section of wax to over-dye or correct a mistake, simply iron the fabric and wax between two pieces of absorbent paper.

6 When completed, wash the fabric thoroughly in hot water to remove all the remaining wax and leave to dry.

Japanese rice resist

1½ hrs   30°–80°C (86°–176°F)

cotton

linen

silk

wool

viscose

mixed fibres

Japanese rice paste is used by Japanese craftspeople as a resist in a technique known as tsutsugaki, literally "cone writing". There are many different ways of preparing the paste, but the following recipe is easy to make and use with ordinary paintbrushes or piping bags. By varying the amounts of water in the recipe, different effects can easily be achieved.

1 Iron your fabric well and using pins or tape to attach it to the printing table (see page 30).

2 In a glass or metal dye-mixing pot, mix the rice powder and cold water together. Turn out and knead well until mixed (as in bread making). Roll to form 2 or 3 sausages.

3 Wearing safety clothing, place the boiling water, the salt, and the sausage-shaped dough in a dye container and simmer for 15 minutes or until the dough rises to the surface.

4 Remove the dough and mix with a small amount of the dye container solution to form a smooth, even paste.

5 In a separate glass or metal mixing pot, carefully add the calcium hydroxide to the cold water. Stir gently to dissolve well. Add this mixture to the dough paste and mix well until it changes to a yellow colour.

6 Using this mixture, paint your design on to the fabric. Alternatively try using a piping bag to apply a pattern. Allow to dry.

7 To colour the fabric, follow the recipe for indigo dye on page 72, blue-grey on page 79, or multi-purpose cold-water dyes on page 88.

8 After dyeing, wash the fabric in warm water with a small amount of mild detergent to remove all traces of the paste. Finally, rinse in cold water and leave to dry.

You will need

- Safety clothing
- Printing table
- Pins or tape
- Glass or metal dye pots for mixing
- Dye container
- Paintbrushes or piping bags
- Iron

Ingredients

- 125g (4½oz) rice flour
- 150ml (⅔ cup) cold water
- 70g (2½oz) household salt
- 5 litres (1 gallon) boiling water
- 40g (1½oz) calcium hydroxide
- 50ml (¼ cup) cold water

cotton

linen

silk

wool

nylon

viscose

polyester

mixed fibres

1 hr   3–5mins

Foil dot

You will need

- Safety clothing
- Pins or tape
- Paintbrush
- Iron

Ingredients

- 100g (4oz) flock adhesive glue or foil adhesive glue
- Textile foil in various colours

Y ou can use metallic foils on almost all kinds of fabrics to produce amazingly visual patterns and designs. The foil is fixed to the fabric by means of adhesive glue, which can be applied by a variety of methods, ranging from painting to stencilling and screen-printing. In this recipe it is applied with a paintbrush to produce a dot pattern.

1 Press the fabric well and, using pins or tape, attach it to your printing table (see page 30).

2 Wearing safety clothing, dip the tip of the paintbrush into the adhesive glue and carefully paint your design onto the fabric. Work from one side of the fabric to the other in order not to smudge the wet glue.

3 When the glue is dry to the touch, immediately place the foil, colour-side uppermost, over the area and, with a hot iron, iron the foil to the fabric. Press firmly to fix the foil to the fabric.

4 After 3 to 5 minutes of ironing, allow the fabric to cool and peel off the excess foil to reveal the foil on the areas to which you applied the glue.

Alternative colourway You can use more than one colour of foil on your fabric by repeating steps 2, 3, and 4, substituting a different coloured foil each time. This build-up of colour is most effective. If using a chiffon fabric, the adhesive glue will go through the fabric, so that both sides can be foiled at the same time, even in different colours.

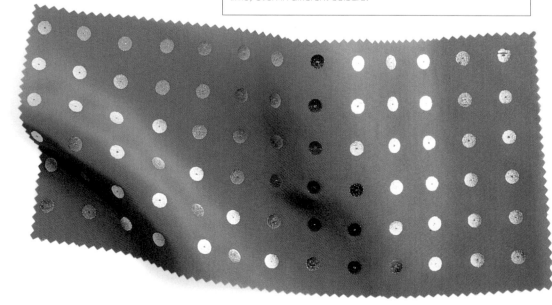

Moorish classic

2 hrs   3–5mins

This classic design with a Moorish touch was created on cotton using reactive dyes. One of industry's most commonly used dyestuffs, reactive dyes are very lightfast and washfast and are available in a wide range of colours. These dyestuffs can also be used on linen, silk and viscose.

1 Press the fabric well and, using pins or tape, attach it to your printing table (see page 30).
2 Wearing safety clothing, first make the thickening binder into a paste by mixing the sodium alginate thickener and the warm water in a glass or plastic dye-mixing pot using an electric hand-mixer or blender.
3 In a glass or metal dye-mixing pot, dissolve the reactive dye powder in the 100ml (½ cup) of hot water, stirring thoroughly to dissolve. While the water is still hot, add the urea and washing soda, stirring well.
4 Add this mixture to the paste mixed in step 1 and then add the wetting out agent. Stir well until a smooth dye paste is formed.
5 In another glass or metal dye-mixing pot, mix the sodium carbonate and the 115ml (½ cup) of cold water and, when dissolved, add this to the dye paste above.
6 Do this for each of the colours required. Kept in airtight containers, these dye paste colours will last 3 to 4 weeks. When the paste becomes runny in consistency, it can no longer be used.
7 Using the dye paste, paint your design on to the fabric, allowing each colour to dry before adding the next. Allow to dry.
8 Now fix the dyes by ironing on the back of the fabric with a hot iron for 3–5 minutes.
9 Rinse in plenty of cold running water, then in hand-hot running water. Then wash again in hand-hot water with a little mild detergent. Wash until the water is clear and all the stiffness of the paste has been removed.
10 Finally, rinse in cold running water and leave to dry.

You will need

- Safety clothing
- Pins or tape
- Paintbrushes
- Glass or plastic dye pots with lids for mixing and storing
- Spatula
- Electric hand-mixer or blender
- Glass or metal dye pots for mixing
- Iron

Ingredients

- 20g (¾oz) sodium alginate thickener
- 200ml (¾ cup) warm water
- 10g (2tsp) reactive dye powder
- 100ml (½cup) hot water
- 50g (1¾oz) urea
- 5g (1tsp) washing soda
- 10ml (2tsp) wetting out agent
- 10g (2tsp) sodium carbonate or sodium bicarbonate
- 115ml (½cup) cold water

* Take extra care when handling the reactive dye powders. Always wear a face mask and add the powder gently to the hot water to prevent splashing.

1½hrs   ½hr

Dandelion portrait

You will need

- Safety clothing
- Pins or tape
- Paintbrushes and spatula
- Glass or plastic dye pots with lids for mixing and storing
- Electric hand-mixer or blender
- Glass or metal dye pots for mixing
- Small steamer

Ingredients

- 30g (1¼oz) modified guar gum
- 250ml (1 cup) warm water
- 15g (½oz) direct dye powder
- 100ml (½ cup) hot water
- 25g (1oz) urea
- 5g (1tsp) washing soda
- 8g (1¾tsp) di-sodium hydrogen phosphate
- 100ml (½ cup) warm water

When thinking about a design or pattern for fabric, everyday objects and images around you are often useful sources of inspiration. This design is inspired by the wonderfully bold photographic images of flowers by Fleur Olby, giving floral fabric a new meaning. This technique works on cotton, linen and viscose fabrics.

1 Press the fabric well and, using pins or tape, attach it to your printing table (see page 30).

2 Wearing safety clothing, make the thickening binder paste by mixing together the modified guar gum and the warm water in a glass or plastic dye-mixing pot using an electric hand-mixer or blender.

3 Place 100ml (½ cup) hot water in another dye-mixing pot and add the direct dye powder to the mixture, stirring thoroughly to dissolve. While the water is still hot, mix in the urea and the washing soda, stirring to dissolve well.

4 Add this mixture to the paste binder mixed in step 1. Stir well until a smooth dye paste is formed.

5 Mix the di-sodium hydrogen phosphate and 100ml (½ cup) of warm water in another dye-mixing pot, stirring to dissolve well. Add this solution to the dye paste above. Stir well again to mix all the ingredients together.

6 Do this for each of the colours required. Kept in airtight containers, these dye paste colours will last from 3 to 4 weeks.

7 Using the dye paste, paint your design onto the fabric, allowing each colour to dry before adding the next. When the design is completed, leave to dry.

8 Now fix the dyes by steaming. Follow the instructions on page 25 and steam for 30 minutes.

9 Rinse carefully in plenty of cold running water to avoid any colour marking undecorated areas. Then wash in hand-hot water with a small amount of mild detergent. Finally, rinse in cold running water and leave to dry.

Silk art

1½hrs   ½hr

Silk painting has been practised for centuries in Asia, particularly in Japan, where intricate designs are painted on to kimono silks. Beautiful effects can be achieved by the intermingling of different colours.

1 Press the fabric well and, using pins or tape, attach it to your printing table (see page 30).

2 Wearing safety clothing, make the thickening binder into a paste by mixing the modified guar gum with 250ml (1 cup) of warm water in a glass or plastic dye-mixing pot using an electric hand mixer or blender.

3 In a separate glass or metal dye-mixing pot, add the acid dye powder colour to the 75ml (⅓ cup) of hot water, stirring well to dissolve. Add the glycerine, stirring thoroughly to dissolve all the mixture.

4 Add the acid dye powder colour and glycerine mixture to the paste mixed in step 2 and stir well.

5 In another glass or metal dye-mixing pot, dissolve the ammonium sulphate in 75ml (⅓ cup) of cold water. Add to the mixture in step 4 and then stir thoroughly until a smooth, even paste is formed.

6 Repeat this process for each of the colours required. Kept in airtight containers, these dye paste colours will last for 2–3 months.

7 Using the paintbrush, paint your design on to the fabric. Allow each colour to dry before painting the next. Leave to dry.

8 Now fix these dyes on to the fabric by steaming. Follow the instructions on page 25 and steam for 30 minutes.

9 Rinse carefully in plenty of cold running water to avoid any unfixed dye staining undecorated areas. Then wash in hand-hot water with a little mild detergent.
Finally, rinse in cold running water and leave to dry.

You will need
- Safety clothing
- Pins or tape
- Glass or plastic dye pots with lids for mixing and storing
- Spatula
- Electric hand-mixer or blender
- Glass or metal dye pots for mixing
- Paintbrush
- Small steamer

Ingredients
- 30g (1¼oz) modified guar gum
- 250ml (1 cup) warm water
- 5g (1tsp) acid dye powder colour
- 75ml (⅓ cup) warm water
- 20ml (4tsp) glycerine
- 12g (¼oz) ammonium sulphate
- 75ml (⅓ cup) cold water

1½hrs ½hr

Painterly effects

You will need

- Safety clothing
- Pins or tape
- Thin plastic or polythene sheet
- Glass or plastic dye pots with lids for mixing and storing
- Electric hand-mixer or blender
- Glass or metal dye pots for mixing
- Paintbrush or airbrush and spatula
- Small steamer

Ingredients

- 18g (⅔oz) modified guar gum
- 150ml (⅔ cup) warm water
- 3g (⅔tsp) acid dye powder colour
- 200ml (½ cup) hot water
- 15ml (3tsp) glycerine
- 20g (¾oz) ammonium sulphate
- 100ml (½ cup) cold water

This recipe shows you how to transfer painting techniques to fabric. You can use these techniques to make exciting background colours and surfaces for more detailed work, or use them on their own to create fine multi-coloured fabrics.

1 Press the fabric well and, using pins or tape, attach it to your printing table (see page 30) on top of a thin plastic or polythene sheet to protect your table.

2 Wearing safety clothing, make the thickening binder into a paste by mixing the modified guar gum with 500ml (2 cups) of warm water in a glass or plastic dye-mixing pot using an electric hand-mixer or blender.

3 Place 200ml (¼ cup) of hot water in a glass or metal dye-mixing pot and add the acid dye powder colour. Add the glycerine, stirring thoroughly to dissolve.

4 Add this dye and glycerine mixture to the thickening paste mixed in step 2 and stir until a smooth paste is formed.

5 In another glass or metal dye-mixing pot, dissolve the ammonium sulphate in 100ml (½ cup) of cold water. Add this solution to the main dye paste and stir until mixed.

6 Do this for each of the colours required. Kept in airtight containers, these dye paste colours will last several months.

7a For a water-colour or colour-washed effect, use a paint brush to wet the fabric with cold water and then, while still wet, brush the mixed acid dye colours quickly onto the surface of the fabric to blend the colours. If necessary, use a brush with cold water to blend different colours into each other. Leave to dry.

7b For an airbrushed effect, use an ink diffuser, a canister airbrush, or plant water spray to spray the acid dye colours over the fabric. Be careful to protect the area around your fabric from excess spray. This method is particularly effective when used with stencils. Leave to dry between colours and then leave to dry before steaming.

8 Now fix the dyes onto the fabric by steaming. Following the instructions on page 25, steam for 30 minutes.

9 After steaming, rinse carefully to avoid unfixed dye staining undecorated areas. Rinse in plenty of cold running water and then wash in hand-hot water with a small amount of mild detergent. Finally, rinse in cold running water and leave to dry.

Salt on silk

1½hrs   ½hr

A wide range of patterns and effects can be obtained by applying either salt or sugar to wet or dry silk. In this recipe, a fine textured finish is produced by applying salt to wet silk.

1 Press the fabric well and, using pins or tape, attach it to your printing table (see page 30) on top of a sheet of thin plastic or polythene to protect your work surface from any excess water used in this recipe.

2 Wearing safety clothing, make up the acid dye in your desired colours as described in the painterly effects recipe on page 120.

3 Use a large decorator's paintbrush to paint the acid dye over the fabric, and while still wet, sprinkle either or both of the salts over the fabric. Leave to dry.

4 Now fix the dyes onto the fabric by steaming. Following the instructions on page 25, steam for 30 minutes.

5 After steaming, rinse carefully to avoid unfixed dye staining undecorated areas. Rinse in plenty of cold running water and then wash in hand-hot water with a small amount of mild detergent. Finally, rinse in cold running water and leave to dry.

Alternative method For a different effect, try dipping the fabric in a strong sugar solution of 500g (18oz) to 2 litres (½ gallon) of warm water. Leave to dry overnight, and then pin out your fabric in the usual way (see page 30) and paint the acid dyes over this coated fabric. You can also make the salt or sugar into a paste form with a small amount of hot water and paint this on to your fabric.

You will need
- Safety clothing
- Pins or tape
- Thin plastic or polythene sheet
- Glass or plastic dye pots with lids for mixing and storing
- Electric hand-mixer or blender
- Glass or metal dye pots for mixing
- Large decorator's paintbrush
- Small steamer

Ingredients
- Fine table salt and/or sea salt
- Acid dye colour ingredients (see page 120)

½hr   ½hr

Acid on nylon

You will need

- Safety clothing
- Pins or tape
- Fine paintbrushes and spatula
- Glass or plastic dye pots with lids for mixing and storing
- Electric hand-mixer or blender
- Glass or metal dye pots for mixing
- Small steamer

Ingredients

- 40g (1½oz) modified guar gum
- 300ml (1⅓ cups) warm water
- 10g (2tsp) acid dye powder colour
- 12ml (2½tsp) glycerine
- 100ml (½ cup) hot water
- 40g (1½oz) urea
- 125ml (½ cup) warm water
- 15g (½oz) ammonium sulphate
- 15g (½oz) sodium carbonate

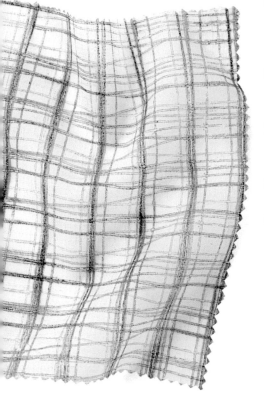

Acid dyes are ideal for nylon fabric, because they colour the fabric without affecting its handling quality. Today there are numerous interesting nylon fabrics available, so use this recipe to experiment with fabrics such as paper nylon or ripstock nylon.

1 Press the fabric well and, using pins or tape, attach it to your printing table (see page 30).

2 Wearing safety clothing, make the thickening binder into a paste by mixing together the modified guar gum and 300ml (1⅓ cups) of warm water with an electric hand-mixer or blender in a glass or plastic dye-mixing pot.

3 In another glass or metal dye-mixing pot, mix the acid dye powder colour with the glycerine. Add 100ml (½ cup) of hot water and stir well until the dye powder is fully dissolved.

4 Put the thickening paste mixed in step 2 in another glass or plastic dye-mixing pot and add the dissolved acid dye. Mix until smooth.

5 In another glass or metal dye-mixing dye pot, dissolve the urea in 125ml (½ cup) of warm water and then add the ammonium sulphate. Add this mixture to the main dye paste and stir until fully mixed.

6 Repeat steps 2 to 5 for each of the colours required. Kept in airtight containers, these dye paste colours will last for two to three months.

7 Using the dye paste, paint your design or pattern on to the fabric, allowing each colour to dry before adding the next. Allow to dry.

8 Now fix the dyes by steaming. Follow the instructions on page 25 and steam for 30 minutes.

9 Wash carefully to avoid any dye marking undecorated areas. Wash first in plenty of cold water containing the sodium carbonate. Then wash in hand-hot water with a small amount of mild detergent. Finally, rinse in cold running water and leave to dry.

Contemporary pastel

1hr   3-5 mins

This recipe uses an acetate stencil to create a stunning repeat motif on light-coloured fabric. An infinite range of pastel colours can be produced by mixing various amounts of pure pigment colours with white pigment colour. These colours are easy to mix so you can pattern fabric to match any modern interior look. This recipe works on almost all fabric types.

1 Press the fabric well and, using pins or tape, attach it to your printing table (see page 30).

2 Wearing safety clothes, mix 10 to 20g (2–4tsp) white pigment colour, depending on the strength of colour required, with the neutral pigment binder in a glass or plastic dye pot. Add tiny amounts of the pure pigment colour to make up the required pastel colour. For example, add a blue for a pale chalky blue, a red for a pale chalky pink, or a black for a grey colour.

3 Now you need to make your acetate stencil. First place a cutting mat or a piece of thick cardboard onto a work surface. If you want to work from a photocopied design or drawing, tape this to the mat or cardboard. Now tape the acetate sheet on top of this and carefully cut out your design using a sharp craft knife.

4 Lightly spray the back of the cut acetate stencil with spray mount adhesive. Place immediately spray-side down onto some spare fabric to remove any excess spray mount and then position the acetate stencil onto the fabric you wish to decorate.

5 Paint your design onto the fabric using the acetate stencil. Allow each colour to dry, then repeat to complete your design.

6 When the design is completed and dry, iron on the back of the fabric with a hot iron for 3 to 5 minutes, pressing firmly to fix the pattern into the fabric.

You will need
- Safety clothing
- Pins or tape
- Acetate sheet
- Craft knife or scissors and spatula
- Cutting mat or thick cardboard
- Light spray mount adhesive
- Glass or plastic dye pots with lids for mixing and storing
- Iron

Ingredients
- 200g (7oz) neutral pigment binder
- 10-20g (2–4tsp) white pigment colour
- 1–6g (¼–1¼tsp) pure pigment colour

cotton

linen

silk

wool

nylon

viscose

polyester

mixed fibres

½hr   chemical
reaction

Indigo stripping

The usual method of creating a pattern on indigo-dyed cloth is to use a resist technique. However, this recipe shows how to use the technique of colour stripping to take away the colour after dyeing to reveal a stunning design.

You will need

- Safety clothing
- Pins or tape
- Glass or plastic dye pots with lids for mixing and storing
- Spatula
- Electric hand-mixer or blender
- Glass or metal dye pots for mixing
- Strainer
- Paintbrush
- Dye container
- Small steamer

Ingredients

- 40g (1½oz) gum tragacanth or starch ether
- 500ml (2 cups) warm water
- 50g (1¾oz) potassium permanganate crystals
- 250ml (1cup) hot water
- 2.5 litres (½ gallon) warm water
- 25ml (5tsp) citric acid
- 2.5 litres (½ gallon) warm water
- 25g (1oz) sodium carbonate

1 Iron the indigo-dyed fabric well and, using pins or tape, attach it to your printing table (see page 30).

2 Wearing safety clothes, make a thickening binder paste by mixing the gum tragacanth or starch ether and warm water in a pot using an electric hand-mixer or blender.

3 In another dye-mixing pot, dissolve the potassium permanganate crystals in the hot water.

4 Add this dissolved mixture to the gum tragcanth paste, straining if necessary.

5 Use the mixture immediately to paint your design onto the indigo cloth. Allow to dry.

6 Wearing rubber gloves, place the citric acid and warm water in a dye container and wash the fabric in this solution for 5 minutes, keeping it submerged at all times. To whiten the design, add a small amount of citric acid and continue washing until the design goes white.

7 Rinse well in cold running water.

8 Refill the dye container with 2.5 litres (½ gallon) of warm water and add the sodium carbonate. Wash the fabric again in this solution for a few minutes to neutralize the effects of the chemicals on the fabric.

9 Finally, rinse well in cold running water and leave to dry.

Wool devoré

1 hr   pressure steam 15 mins

wool

wool mix

While you would normally avoid making holes in fabric, here, by using a devoré mixture, a wonderful pattern is created on this woollen fabric. You can also use this recipe to devoré wool-mix fabric, taking the wool away and leaving just the polyester or cotton fibres.

1 Press the fabric well and, using pins or tape, attach it to your printing table (see page 30).

2 Wearing safety clothing, make the thickening binder into a paste by mixing the starch ether with the 350ml (1½ cups) of warm water in a glass dye-mixing pot using an electric hand-mixer or blender.

3 Very carefully, to avoid any splashing, add the sodium hydroxide solution 72°TW to the mixed thickening paste, stirring gently to mix. This mixture will produce heat as it is mixed together, so leave to cool before using.

4 Using the paintbrush, paint your design onto the fabric with the paste mixed in step 3. You will need to paint it quite thickly to ensure that the paste penetrates the fibres well. Leave to dry.

5 Now fix the paste onto the fabric by pressure steaming. Follow the instructions on page 25 and pressure steam for 15 minutes with 2lb of pressure.

6 Place 10ml (2tsp) cold water in a glass dye-mixing pot and carefully add the acetic acid. Always add acid to water, never water to acid.

7 After steaming, wash the fabric carefully to remove the paste. First, wash in hot water for 15 to 20 minutes to finish devouring away the wool fibres. Wash again in warm water containing the acetic acid solution to neutralize the effects of the sodium hydroxide. Then wash in warm water with a small amount of mild detergent. Finally, rinse in cold running water and leave to dry.

You will need

- Safety clothing
- Pins or tape
- Glass dye pots with lids for mixing and storing
- Electric hand-mixer or blender
- Paintbrush and spatula
- Small pressure cooker for steaming

Ingredients

- 35g (1⅓oz) starch ether
- 350ml (1½ cups) warm water
- 125ml (½ cup) sodium hydroxide solution 72°TW
- 2ml (½tsp) acid acetic 80% tech
- 10ml (2tsp) cold water

Take extreme care at every stage to ensure that no caustic solution comes into contact with your skin. Wear full safety clothing, including eye goggles, rubber gloves and apron, at all times. If the solution comes into contact with your skin, wash immediately with plenty of cold running water for 15 to 20 minutes. If the irritation continues, seek medical advice.

½hr   pressure-steam 20 mins

Polyester painting

You will need

- Safety clothing
- Pins or tape
- Electric hand mixer or blender
- Glass or plastic dye pots with lids for mixing and storing
- Glass or metal dye pots for mixing
- Paintbrushes and spatula
- Pressure cooker

Ingredients

- 40g (1½oz) modified guar gum
- 300ml (1⅓ cups) warm water
- 1ml (¼tsp) citric acid
- 5ml (1tsp) wetting agent
- 10ml (2tsp) wetting out agent
- 10g (2tsp) disperse dye powder colour
- 25ml (5tsp) polythene glycol 200
- 150ml (⅔ cup) warm water

With the ever-growing range of fabrics manufactured today from synthetic fibres such as polyester, so the need for suitable methods of decorating them increases. This recipe is for a coloured paste which can be painted onto these fabrics to create your own beautiful textile

1 Press the fabric well and, using pins or tape, attach it to your printing table (see page 30).

2 Wearing safety clothing, make the thickening binder into a paste by mixing together the modified guar gum and 300ml (1⅓ cups) of warm water in a glass or plastic dye-mixing pot using an electric hand-mixer or blender.

3 Add the citric acid, wetting agent, and wetting out agent to the binder paste and mix well.

4 In another glass or metal dye-mixing pot, mix together the disperse dye powder colour and the polythene glycol 200. Add 150ml (⅔ cup) of warm water and stir thoroughly.

5 Add the two mixtures together in a glass or plastic dye-mixing pot and stir well to form a smooth paste. Repeat steps 2 to 5 for each of the colours required. Kept in air-tight containers, these dye paste colours will last for several weeks.

6 Using the dye paste, paint your design or pattern on to the fabric, allowing each colour to dry before adding the next. Allow to dry.

7 Now fix the dyes by steaming. Follow the instructions on page 25 and pressure-steam for 20 minutes with 2lb of pressure.

8 Rinse carefully in cold running water to avoid any dyestuff marking undecorated areas. Then wash in hand-hot water with a small amount of mild detergent. Finally, rinse in cold running water and leave to dry.

Flock fabric

1hr   45-60 secs

cotton
linen
silk
wool
nylon
viscose
polyester
mixed fibres

Flocking paper was developed by the T-shirt industry as a safer and more controllable medium than flocking fibres, and it can now be seen in some exclusive designer collections. In this recipe, the flock is fixed to the fabric with flocking glue applied with a stiff brush to produce a textural effect.

You will need
- Safety clothing
- Pins or tape
- Stiff paintbrush
- Iron

Ingredients
- Flocking paper
- 100g (4oz) flocking glue

1 Flocking paper is generally manufactured in black and white, which you can also colour yourself. To colour the paper, follow the instructions on page 79 for grey-blue. Dip the paper into the dye container for a few minutes only to colour, and leave to dry.

2 Press the fabric well and, using pins or tape, attach it to your printing table (see page 30).

3 Wearing safety clothing, dip the tip of a stiff brush into the flocking glue and lightly brush the fabric with glue to deposit a small, thin layer of glue across the surface. Leave until dry to the touch.

4 Place the flocking paper flock-side down on top of the glued fabric, and iron firmly on to the fabric with a hot iron for 45 to 60 seconds. Lift a corner of the paper to see if the flocking fibres have transferred to the fabric. Iron again if necessary.

5 You can apply several colours of flock by repeating this process using different-coloured flocking papers each time.

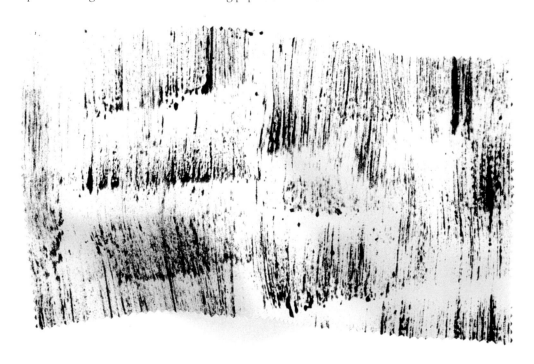

1 day   ½hr

Gutta graffiti

You will need

- Safety clothing
- Wooden frame to fit your fabric
- Drawing pins (thumbtacks)
- Glass or plastic dye pots with lids for mixing and storing
- Plastic bottle with small nozzle or pipette
- Paintbrushes and spatula
- Small steamer

Ingredients

- Ready-mixed gutta, either coloured or metallic
- 1g (¼tsp) acid dye powder colour
- 200ml (¾ cup) hot water
- 5ml (1tsp) glycerine
- 5g (1tsp) ammonium sulphate

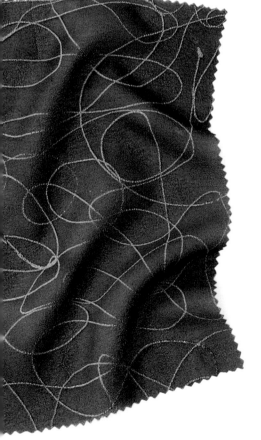

Gutta is probably one of the earliest methods of producing line work on fine wools, cottons and silk. It is also one the first methods that people choose to use when decorating fabric, because it is readily available in craft stores. In this recipe I've used ready-made gutta, but combined it with acid dye powder colours to make a stunning design on silk. Note that fabrics decorated with gutta cannot be dry-cleaned, because the gutta will be erased by the solvents used in the cleaning process.

1 Pin out the fabric on an open wooden frame, such as an old picture frame or artist's stretcher bars. Using drawing pins (thumb tacks), start in the middle of the longest side and attach the fabric to the frame with three pins at intervals of 5cm (2in). Repeat this process on the opposite side, pulling the fabric taught across the frame. Do the same to the two shorter sides, and then continue to pin and stretch all the way around the frame, working from alternate sides each time.

2 Using either a plastic bottle with a small nozzle, a pipette, or a fine paintbrush, apply the gutta to the stretched silk. Do remember that the line design that you draw must enclose into separate areas so you are able to colour these areas without contaminating other areas. Leave the fabric on the frame to dry overnight.

3 Wearing safety clothing, place the hot water in a glass or plastic dye-mixing pot and mix in the acid dye powder colour, stirring thoroughly so no lumps remain. Add the glycerine and ammonium sulphate and stir well to dissolve. Leave to cool.

4 Do this for each colour required. Kept in airtight containers, these dyes will last for several months.

5 Paint the dye colours onto the areas outlined by the gutta and leave to dry.

6 Now fix the dyes onto the fabric by steaming. Following the instructions on page 25, steam for 30 minutes.

7 After steaming, wash carefully to avoid any unfixed dye staining undecorated areas. Rinse in plenty of cold running water and then wash in hand-hot water with a small amount of mild detergent. Finally, rinse in cold running water and leave to dry.

Vat illuminated colours

The most expensive printing effects on clothing ranges by top designers are created using vat dyes. Although a common fault in the process is the formation of haloeing around the design, this characteristic can be deliberately incorporated into your design. This recipe will work on cotton, viscose, and silk–viscose velvet.

1 Press your fabric well and, using pins or tape, attach it to your printing table (see page 30).

2 Wearing safety clothing, make the thickening binder into a paste by mixing the starch ether and the cold water in a glass or plastic dye-mixing pot using an electric hand-mixer or blender.

3 In another glass or metal dye-mixing pot, mix the vat dye powder colour with the glycerine. By varying the amount of dye powder, you can obtain paler or stronger shades. Add the hot water and stir to dissolve.

4 Add this mixture to the paste binder mixed in step 2. Stir well to form a smooth dye paste.

5 Now add the reducing agent, the potassium carbonate, and the sodium carbonate. Mix well using an electric hand-mixer or blender until a smooth paste is formed.

6 Repeat steps 2 to 5 for each colour required. These dye pastes will last only for a few days in airtight containers.

7 Using the dye paste, paint your design or pattern onto the fabric, allowing each colour to dry before adding the next. If using silk-viscose velvet, apply to the pile side of the fabric. Allow to dry.

8 Now fix the dyes by steaming. Follow the instructions on page 25 and steam for 15 to 20 minutes.

9 After steaming, rinse carefully in cold running water to avoid any dye marking undecorated areas. Wash in cold water containing the hydrogen peroxide solution to oxidize the colours and then in hand-hot water with a little mild detergent. Finally, rinse in cold running water and leave to dry.

Alternative colourway Note that only a limited range of vat dye powder colours will work in this way. The following vat dye powders will produce good results: vat yellow 2 or 4, vat orange 1 or 7, vat red 1 or 14, vat violet 1or 3, vat blue 4 or 5, vat green 1 or 3, vat brown 57, Solanthrene printing black.

You will need

- Safety clothing
- Pins or tape
- Paintbrushes and spatula
- Glass or plastic dye pots with lids for mixing and storing
- Electric hand-mixer or blender
- Glass or metal dye pots for mixing
- Small steamer

Ingredients

- 30g (1¼oz) starch ether
- 300ml (1⅓cups) cold water
- 3–8g (⅔–1¾tsp) vat dye powder colour
- 5ml (1tsp) glycerine
- 50ml (¼ cup) hot water
- 80g (3oz) sodium formaldehyde sulphoxylate (reducing agent)
- 25g (1oz) potassium carbonate
- 25g (1oz) sodium carbonate
- 20ml (4tsp) hydrogen peroxide solution

1½ hrs   5-10 mins

Woollen relief

You will need

- Safety clothing
- Pins or tape
- Glass or plastic dye pots with lids for mixing and storing
- Electric hand-mixer or blender
- Glass or metal dye pots for mixing
- Paintbrush and spatula
- Greaseproof paper
- Iron

Ingredients

- 7g (1½ tsp) sodium alginate thickener
- 150ml (⅔ cup) warm water
- 30ml (6tsp) Synthappret BAP
- 8g (1¾ tsp) sodium carbonate
- 10ml (2tsp) wetting agent
- 300ml (1⅓ cups) cold water

W e all know how easy it is to make a mistake and felt your favourite wool sweater in a hot wash. However, this simple recipe uses this well-known characteristic of wool to great effect to create a fabulous textured design instead.

1 Press the fabric well and, using pins or tape, attach it to your printing table (see page 30).

2 Wearing full safety clothing, make the thickening binder into a paste form by mixing the sodium alginate thickener with 150ml (⅔ cup) warm water in a glass or plastic dye-mixing pot using an electric hand-mixer or blender.

3 Add the Synthappret BAP, sodium carbonate, wetting agent, and 300ml (1⅓ cups) of cold water to this mixture, stirring well until a smooth paste is formed.

4 Use the paste to paint your design onto the fabric. Apply it quite thickly, making sure it penetrates the fabric – go over the design again if necessary. The painted areas will remain unfelted in the final design. Leave to dry.

5 Cover the fabric with greaseproof paper and, using a hot iron, press for 5 to 10 minutes, taking care that the fabric does not burn.

6 Wash the fabric in hot water with a little mild detergent for 20 to 30 minutes or until all the unpainted areas felt. Finally, rinse in cold water and leave to dry.

Crinkled crepon

W hen the chemicals used in wool devoré are used on unmercerized cotton (unfinished cotton), a crinkled textural effect known as crepon is produced. The best results are achieved by covering around 50 per cent of the fabric with your design, leaving the rest free of paste.

1 Press the fabric well and, using pins or tape, attach it to your printing table (see page 30).
2 Wearing safety clothing, make the thickening binder into a paste by mixing the starch ether and warm water in a glass dye-mixing pot using an electric hand-mixer or blender.
3 Taking care to avoid splashing, add the sodium hydroxide solution 72°TW to the thickening paste and stir gently to mix. This mixture will produce heat as it is mixed together so you will need to leave to cool before using.
4 On a cutting board, cut your design into the acetate sheet using a scalpel (xacto knife). Place the acetate design on your fabric and apply the paste thickly.
5 Remove the fabric from the table while still wet and leave to dry for 1 to 2 hours. The design will shrink.
6 Put 10ml (2tsp) of cold water in a glass pot and add the acetic acid. Always add acid to water, never water to acid.
7 Rinse the fabric in cold water for 3 to 5 minutes. To neutralize the effects of the sodium hydroxide, wash in warm water containing the acetic acid solution. Finally, wash in warm water with mild detergent, rinse, and dry.

You will need

- Safety clothing
- Pins or tape
- Glass dye-mixing pots with lids for mixing and storing
- Electric hand-mixer or blender
- Cutting board or thick cardboard
- Scalpel (xacto knife)
- Sheet of acetate
- Paintbrush

Ingredients

- 35g (1⅓oz) starch ether
- 350ml (1½ cups) warm water
- 125ml (½ cup) sodium hydroxide solution 72°TW
- 2ml (½tsp) acid acetic 80% tech
- 10ml (2tsp) cold water

Take extreme care at every stage to ensure that no caustic solution comes into contact with your skin. Wear full safety clothing, including eye goggles, rubber gloves and apron, at all times. If the solution comes into contact with your skin, wash immediately with plenty of cold running water for 15 to 20 minutes. If the irritation continues, seek medical advice.

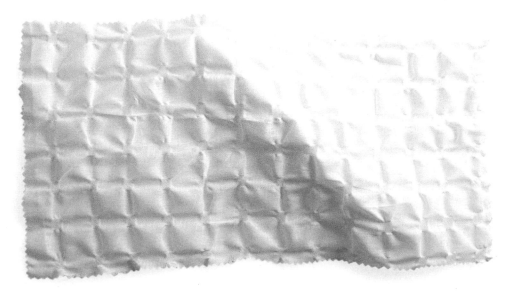

4 hrs   40°-80°C
               (104°-176°F)

Wax crackle

You will need

- Safety clothing
- Pins or tape
- A large and a small metal dye pot for mixing
- Decorator's stiff brush
- Blunt knife
- Brown paper
- Iron

Ingredients

- 150-250ml (⅔–1 cup) boiling water
- 200g (7oz) paraffin wax or beeswax, or a mixture of the two
- Cold-water reactive dying recipe (see page 79)

The well-known resist technique of batik is just one of the many methods of applying hot wax to decorate fabric. In this recipe, the fabric is painted all over with hot wax and then folded so that lines of fabric are revealed where the wax cracks. Dye can then be applied to these areas to create an unusual design on your fabric.

1 Press the fabric well and, using pins or tape, attach it to your printing table (see page 30).
2 Wearing safety clothing, place the boiling water in the larger metal dye-mixing pot. Put the wax in the smaller pot and place this pot in the larger pot. Heat gently on an electric or gas ring until the wax has liquefied.
3 Using the decorator's stiff brush, paint the liquefied wax all over the fabric. Leave to cool until wax is hard.
4 Fold the waxed fabric into sections so that the wax cracks to reveal the fabric underneath. Using the cold-water reactive dyeing recipe on page 79, dip the fabric into the container to colour the lines. Remove the fabric and allow to dry.
5 Using a blunt knife, carefully scrape off the wax.Then place the fabric between two sheets of brown paper and, using a hot iron, press well to remove any remaining wax.
6 If any wax still remains, boil the fabric in water with a small amount of mild detergent for 5 to 10 minutes. Finally rinse in warm water and leave to dry.

Textured effect

1hr   10-15 mins

cotton
linen
silk
wool
nylon
viscose
polyester
mixed fibres

This recipe uses puff binder to produce amazing sculptural effects on flat fabric. First used in T-shirt and sweatshirt printing, this binder is a surface pigment, so it can be used on almost all fabric types. Try this recipe on sheer or very lightweight fabrics – you will find that you can alter the handling quality and the way in which fabrics hang considerably by applying a pattern over large areas of the piece. The puff binder can be used on its own to produce a cream-coloured pattern, but you can also create a range of coloured, raised surfaces and textures on your fabric.

You will need
- Safety clothing
- Pins or tape
- Glass or plastic dye pots with lids for mixing and storing
- Paintbrushes and spatula
- Hair dryer

Ingredients
- 200g (7oz) puff pigment binder
- 2-6g (⅓–1¼tsp) pure pigment colour

1 Press the fabric well and, using pins or tape, attach it to your printing table (see page 30).
2 Wear safety clothing. According to the strength of colour required, mix 2–6g (⅓–1¼tsp) pure pigment colour with the puff pigment binder in a glass or plastic dye pot.
3 Paint the design or pattern as required onto your fabric. By using different sizes of paintbrush, you can vary the textural effects obtained with the puff binder. Leave to dry
4 .Use a hair dryer on a hot setting directed at the fabric for 10 to 15 minutes to make the binder rise. Take care not to burn the fabric while raising the binder.

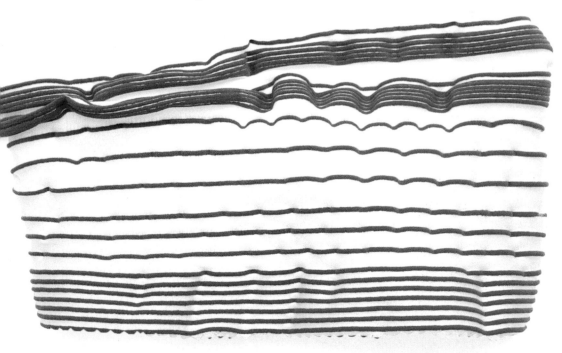

2 hrs 10 mins

Colour-stripped silk

You will need

- Safety clothing
- Pins and masking tape
- Glass or plastic dye pots with lids for mixing and storing
- Electric hand-mixer or blender
- Paintbrush and scissors
- Small steamer

Ingredients

- 30g (1¼oz) modified guar gum
- 250ml (1 cup) warm water
- 100g (4oz) zinc formaldehyde sulphoxylate (reducing agent)
- 20ml (4tsp) glycerine
- 180ml (⅔ cup) cold water

In this recipe, masking tape is used as a resist device to achieve a particularly bold effect. By cutting the tape into a wavy shape, it becomes less obvious exactly how the design was put onto the fabric. The strong contrast of colours is created by first dyeing the silk with a fully discharged dye powder colour.

1 Press the fabric well and, using pins or tape, attach it to your printing table (see page 30).

2 Wearing safety clothing, make the thickening binder into a paste by mixing the modified guar gum and 250ml (1 cup) of warm water in a glass or plastic dye-mixing pot using an electric hand-mixer or blender.

3 Add the reducing agent, glycerine and 180ml (¼cup) of cold water to this paste and stir thoroughly, or mix with an electric hand-mixer or blender until a smooth paste is formed.

4 Cut strips of masking tape to form wavy stripes and stick them in position on the fabric, pressing down well. Using a paint brush, paint an even layer of the mixed paste onto the fabric. Allow to dry, but leave for no longer than 1 to 2 hours, because this this will affect the final results. The colour will be unevenly stripped away from the painted areas. Remove the masking tape.

5 Now fix the dye by steaming. Follow the instructions on page 25 and steam for 10 minutes.

6 After steaming, wash carefully to avoid any unfixed paste staining undecorated areas. Rinse in plenty of cold running water and then wash in hand-hot water with a small amount of mild detergent. Finally, rinse in cold running water and leave to dry.

Pigment stripes

1hr   3-5 mins

The best way to create a white design on a dark background is to use pigment colour dyes. Unlike many commercial oil-based inks, these dyes do not create a thick, heavy layer of stiff ink on the fabric. This recipe works on almost all fabric types.

1 Press the fabric well and, using pins or tape, attach it to your printing table (see page 30).
2 Wear safety clothing throughot this recipe. Now you need to make up a binder mix, because the opaque pigment binder cannot be used on its own as it is too heavy, and excessive amounts will not fix to the fabric. To make the mix, add the neutral pigment binder to the opaque pigment binder in a glass or plastic dye-mixing pot.
3 For a pure colour, add the pure pigment colour to your binder mix according to strength of colour required. If you want a more pastel colour, mix in the white pigment colour according to strength of colour required.
4 Stick masking tape directly on to your fabric to create a design or pattern. This technique is ideal for linear designs – try stripes, a grid, or blocks of colour.
5 Paint the mixed pigment colour onto the uncovered areas of the fabric, leaving each colour to dry before applying a new one. You can add and take away tape to build up the design or pattern. Leave to dry. Remove the masking tape.
6 When the design is completely dry, iron on the back of the fabric with a hot iron for 3 to 5 minutes, pressing firmly to fix the pattern into the fabric.

Alternative method The proportions of neutral pigment binder and opaque pigment binder can be varied depending on the darkness of your fabric. This recipe is for a very dark fabric and uses a 50:50 mix of binders. For lighter fabrics, decrease the opaque pigment binder and increase the neutral pigment binder.

You will need

- Safety clothing
- Pins and masking tape
- Glass dye pots with lids for mixing and storing
- Paintbrushes and Spatula
- Masking tape
- Iron

Ingredients

- 100g (4oz) neutral pigment binder
- 100g (4oz) opaque pigment binder
- 2-6g (⅓–1¼tsp) pure pigment colour
- 10-20g (2–4tsp) white pigment colour (for pastel colour)

cotton

linen

silk

wool

nylon

viscose

polyester

mixed fibres

1 hr   2-3 mins

Glitter look

You will need

- Safety clothing
- Pins or tape
- Paintbrushes
- Baking paper or teflon-coated paper
- iron

Ingredients

- Glitter binder adhesive glue
- Glitter powder

Glitter powder creates a fabulous sparkling effect which is guaranteed to transform any design into a real party piece. It is particularly effective when used to highlight a small section of a design along with another patterning recipe. If you like this look, try experimenting on different types of fabric with the many different sizes and colours of glitter powder available .

1 Press the fabric well and, using pins or tape, attach it to your printing table (see page 30).

2 Wearing safety clothing, paint the adhesive glue onto the fabric, either to create your own design in glitter, or to highlight with glitter a fabric that is already patterned.

3 While the adhesive glue is still wet, sprinkle the glitter powder over the glued areas. Take care because the powder does scatter easily and, although it will stick only onto the glued fabric, it can be difficult to clean up.

4 Remove the fabric from the printing table and shake off any excess glitter onto a sheet of paper. Return the excess glitter to the glitter powder container for re-use.

5 Allow the fabric to dry for about 20 to 30 minutes, then cover with a protective sheet of baking paper or teflon-coated paper and press with a hot iron for 2 to 3 minutes to fix the glitter and adhesive glue onto your fabric.

Alternative colourway Try mixing two or more glitter colours together before sprinkling them onto the wet adhesive glue. For a more controlled colour differentiation, apply glue in stages, glittering each section as you go to complete the finished design.

Devoré velvet

1½hrs   1 min

Devoré velvet has traditionally been regarded as a luxury fabric. However, as fabric production costs decrease and as more two-fibre fabrics are woven, the possibilities for using the devoré technique increase. You can use this recipe to devoré silk/viscose or polyester/cotton velvet. You will find that some velvet fabrics devoré well, while others leave interesting woven-thread patterns that you can incorporate into your design.

1 Press the fabric well and, using pins or tape, attach the velvet pile-down to your printing table (see page 30). Remember that to devoré a fabric, you must work on the reverse side.

2 Wearing safety clothing, make the thickening binder into a paste by mixing the modified guar gum and the warm water in a glass or plastic dye-mixing pot using an electric hand-mixer or blender.

3 Now add the glycerine, tartaric acid and aluminium sulphate to the thickening paste, and then stir in the cold water. Stir thoroughly for several minutes to mix all the ingredients together to make up the devoré paste.

4 Using clean newsprint or thin cartridge paper, cut out a design to form a stencil for transferring your design to the fabric. Now lightly attach the stencil to the fabric using the lightest quality spray adhesive. Don't forget that the design needs to be a mirror image, because you are working on the back of the fabric.

5 With the devoré paste paint your design using the stencil. Try to apply an even amount of paste throughout, with no thick blobs, because these will devoré more and may cause holes in your fabric later when ironing. Allow to dry thoroughly.

6 Wearing a protective mask and gloves, press the back of the fabric with a hot iron for 30 seconds to 1 minute. When the fabric changes colour from white to pale cream, the burn-out process has occurred. In a well-ventilated area, carefully rub the pile side of the fabric and the devoréd areas will come away to reveal your design.

7 When nearly all the paste is out – a stiff residue is usually left behind after rubbing – wash the fabric in warm water with a small amount of mild detergent. Rinse in cold running water and leave to dry.

You will need

- Safety clothing
- Pins or tape
- Glass or plastic dye pots with lids for mixing and storage
- Electric hand-mixer or blender
- Glass or metal dye pots for mixing
- Newsprint or thin cartridge paper
- Craft knife and cutting board
- Spray adhesive
- Paintbrushes and spatula
- Small steamer

Ingredients

- 30g (1¼oz) modified guar gum
- 250ml (1cup) warm water
- 10ml (2tsp) glycerine
- 20g (4tsp) tartaric acid
- 80g (¾oz) aluminium sulphate
- 100ml (½ cup) cold water

printing

By printing with blocks or silkscreens onto fabric you can cover a large area of fabric rapidly with your design. All the recipes in this section will cover one square metre (nine square feet) of fabric.

cotton
linen
silk
wool
nylon
viscose
polyester
mixed fibres

1½ hrs   3-5 mins

Leafy print

You will need

- Safety clothing
- Pins or tape
- Glass or plastic dye pots with lids for mixing and storing
- Spatula
- Assorted dry leaves
- Sheets of newspaper
- Sheet of acetate, plastic or glass approximately A4 size
- 2 rubber rollers
- Iron

Ingredients

- 2–6g (⅓–1¼tsp) pure pigment colour
- 200g (7oz) neutral pigment binder

In this recipe, the delicate shapes of natural leaves and stems are printed onto fabric using pigment dyes. Closest in type to ordinary paints, these dyes generally consist of a binder and colour mixed together. Best of all, they are simple to use and extremely easy to apply.

1 Press the fabric well and, using pins or tape, attach it to your printing table (see page 30).

2 Wearing safety clothing, make up the pigment paste by mixing the neutral pigment binder and the pure pigment colour in a glass or plastic dye-mixing pot. For a paler, more transparent colour, add just the tiniest amount of pigment on the end of a teaspoon to the neutral pigment binder. To increase the depth of colour, simply add more pigment in tiny amounts.

3 Mix all the colours you want to use in the same way in separate glass or plastic containers.

4 Now place the leaves on the newspaper. Place a small amount of the colour pigment mix onto the acetate, plastic, or glass sheet. Spread out the colour pigment using one rubber roller so that a thin layer of colour is evenly distributed all over the sheet. Press the leaves onto this sheet to pick up the colour and then carefully transfer each coloured leaf onto your fabric. Now use the clean rubber roller to press the leaves firmly but carefully, and transfer the colour and design to your fabric.

5 Allow the dye to dry before adding new colours so that the edges of the leaf prints are crisp and well defined.

6 Leave to dry and then iron the back of the fabric with a hot iron for 3 to 5 minutes, pressing firmly to fix the pattern into the fabric.

Alternative colourway One way to achieve a good mix of colours that work well visually with each other is to use a small amount of the first colour in the second colour and either the first or second colour in the third colour and so on, thus linking together all the colours used.

Velvet effect

1 day   10-15 mins

A marvellous velvet-like texture can be created on fabric by using a flocking gun. Widely used in the textile industry, this tool is available to hire and simple to use, and the flocking fibres come in a wide range of colours.

1 Press the fabric well and, using pins or tape, attach it to your printing table (see page 30). Place newsprint around the edges of the fabric to collect any excess flocking fibres.

2 Wearing safety clothing, screenprint your design onto the fabric using the textile flocking adhesive, pulling the glue across the screen 2 to 3 times. Quickly wash the screen and squeegee thoroughly in running water.

3 Following the manufacturer's instructions carefully at all times and still wearing safety clothing, including a face mask, attach the earth lead of the flocking gun to some suitable earthed metal. Load the flocking gun with the flocking fibres and, while the glue on the fabric is still wet, cover the glued area with flock.

4 When you have finished flocking, leave to dry. Remove the fabric from the table and carefully shake the excess fibres onto the newsprint. Leave to stand overnight.

5 Use a hair dryer on the hot setting directed at the fabric for 10–15 minutes to heat-cure the flocking fibres onto the fabric. Take care not to burn the fabric.

You will need
- Safety clothing
- Pins or tape
- Newsprint
- Flocking gun
- Ready-to-use silkscreen (see page 50)
- Squeegee

Ingredients
- 500g (18oz) flocking adhesive, washfast or dry-cleanable
- 500g (18oz) flocking fibres

cotton

linen

silk

wool

nylon

viscose

polyester

mixed fibres

1hr   3-5 mins

Transfer squares

You can achieve a range of strong colours on synthetic fabrics by using transfer dyes. The simple technique used in this recipe is employed by fabric manufacturers to produce fabric for overalls and uniforms.

You will need
- Safety clothing
- Pins or tape
- Glass or metal dye pots for mixing
- Paintbrushes
- Sheets of plain paper
- Iron

Ingredients
- Ready-mixed transfer dyes or 2–5g (⅓–1tsp) disperse dye powder
- 50ml (¼ cup) boiling water

1 Press the fabric well and, using pins or tape, attach it to your printing table (see page 30).

2 Wear safety clothing throughout the following procedures. If using ready-mixed transfer dyes, these can be used immediately. To mix up your own transfer dyes, add the disperse dye powder to the boiling water in a glass or metal dye-mixing pot and dissolve thoroughly. The amount of disperse dye powder can vary depending on the depth of colour required. Mix all the colours required in separate glass or metal dye-mixing pots.

3 On a separate work surface, paint your design onto sheets of plain paper. Remember that because this is a transfer technique, you should paint your design or pattern as a mirror image. Different sheets of paper can carry different colour elements of the design. Allow to dry.

4 Lay the paper painted-side down on top of the fabric and press firmly with a hot iron for 3 to 5 minutes.

5 Remove the paper and your design will have been transferred to the fabric by the heat and pressure of the iron. Repeat the process to build up more colours or design areas. This repeat process can create interesting overlapping colours.

Wire and polyester

1hr   3-5 mins

This unusual effect is created with a simple resist technique using wire and was first popularized by the British textile designer Rebecca Early. Note that this technique works only on polyester fabrics.

1 Press the fabric well and, using pins or tape, attach it to your printing table (see page 30).

2 If using ready-mixed transfer dyes, these can be used immediately. To mix up your own transfer dyes, wear safety clothing. Add the disperse dye powder to the boiling water in a glass or metal dye-mixing pot and dissolve thoroughly. The amount of disperse dye powder can vary depending on the depth of colour required. Mix all the colours required in separate glass or metal dye-mixing pots.

3 On a separate work surface, paint sheets of plain paper thinly all over with the transfer dye. Leave to dry.

4 Place the fine wire on top of your fabric according to your design. You can also use leaves, washers or even paper shapes to create a resist pattern.

5 Now lay the paper, painted-side down, in contact with the fabric and press firmly with a hot iron for 3 to 5 minutes.

6 Remove the paper and wire, and your design or pattern will be revealed. Further colours and patterns can be built up by repeating the process.

You will need

- Safety clothing
- Pins or tape
- Brushes
- Fine wire in different thicknesses
- Glass or metal dye pots for mixing
- Sheets of plain paper
- Iron

Ingredients

- Ready-mixed transfer dyes or 2-5g (⅓–1tsp) disperse dye powder
- 50ml (¼ cup) boiling water

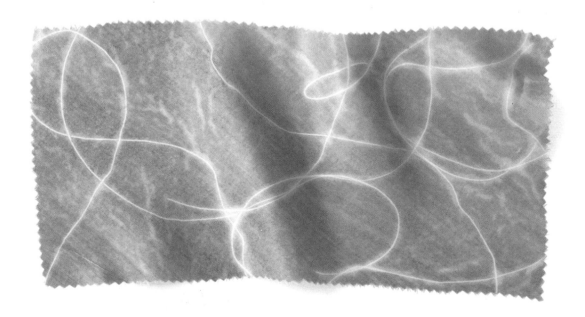

1½hrs   10 mins

Stripped leaves

You will need

- Safety clothing
- Pins or tape
- Glass or plastic dye pots with lids for mixing and storing
- Electric hand-mixer or blender
- Glass or metal dye pots for mixing
- Silkscreen
- Small steamer
- Iron

Ingredients

- 6g (1¼tsp) modified guar gum
- 40ml (3tbsp) hot water
- 375g (13oz) neutral pigment binder
- 40g (1½oz) zinc formaldehyde sulphoxylate (reducing agent)
- 40ml (3tbsp) cold water
- 2–5g (⅓–1tsp) pure pigment colour

This unusual recipe combines two different techniques – colour stripping and pigment colour dyeing – on a cotton fabric. Using these techniques you can add colour to a design area of coloured fabric without needing to use dye powder colours. However, note that only certain pure pigment colours will work with this recipe. Be sure to test first that the colour can be stripped away from your coloured fabric and that your pigment colour will dye your fabric.

1 Press the fabric well and, using pins or tape, attach it to your printing table (see page 30).

2 Wearing safety clothing, make the thickening binder into a paste by mixing together the modified guar gum and the warm water in a glass or plastic dye-mixing pot, using an electric hand-mixer or blender.

3 In another glass or plastic dye-mixing pot, mix the paste with the neutral pigment binder, stirring well.

4 Place the cold water in another glass or metal dye-mixing pot and add the reducing agent, stirring constantly to dissolve thoroughly.

5 Add this solution to the binder mix and mix together using a small electric hand-mixer or blender.

6 Carefully stir in the pure pigment colour, adding more to give a stronger colour as desired. Do this for each of the colours required. Note that these dye paste colours will last only for a few days in airtight containers, because they contain the reducing agent (zinc formaldehyde sulphoxylate).

7 Following the instructions on page 50, screenprint your design onto the fabric using the dye pastes, allowing each colour to dry before applying the next.

8 These dyes now need to be fixed onto the fabric by steaming. Follow the instructions on page 25 and steam for 10 minutes. In a well-ventilated area and wearing a face mask, iron the back of the fabric for 1 to 2 minutes to finish fixing the colours to the fabric.

9 Wash in lukewarm water until the water runs clear and the fabric returns to its original handling quality. Leave to dry.

Rowan blueprinting

1½hrs   10-15 mins

cotton

linen

silk

Blueprinting, or cyanotype, is a simple photographic process that can be carried out in the home without a darkroom. This technique can be used on fabric to produce a very detailed classic blueprint image highlighted in white against a blue background. The best results can be achieved using fresh flowers, leaves, or feathers, but try experimenting with other objects such as glass fragments or acetate photocopies.

1 Wearing safety clothing, dissolve the ammonium ferric citrate in 125ml (½ cup) cold water in a glass dye-mixing pot and stir well with a plastic spoon until fully dissolved.
2 In another glass dye-mixing pot dissolve the potassium ferric cyanide in 125ml (½ cup) of cold water and stir well with a plastic spoon until fully dissolved.
3 Mix the two solutions together, stirring thoroughly.
4 Cover the cardboard or wooden board with several sheets of newspaper and then lightly tape the fabric onto the board.
5 In a darkened room, paint the solution mixed in step 2 evenly over the fabric and allow to dry.
6 Place your flowers, leaves or feathers on top of the painted fabric, and cover with the glass or plastic sheet.
7 Either open the curtains and let the sunlight in for 20 to 30 minutes, depending on the strength of the light, or take the board outside and expose to direct sunlight for 10 to 15 minutes. By experimenting with the amount of sunlight the fabric is exposed to, you can obtain different shades of blue.
8 To develop and reveal the image, remove the glass or plastic sheet and rinse the fabric under cold running water until the water runs clear. Leave to dry. (Note that this fabric can be dry cleaned only or washed in cold water with no detergent.)

You will need
- Safety clothing
- Plastic spoons
- Glass dye-mixing pots
- Tape
- Flat cardboard or wooden board the same size as your fabric
- Flowers, leaves or feathers
- Sheet of glass or plastic the same size as your fabric
- Paintbrush
- Newspaper

Ingredients
- 32g (1¼oz) ammonium ferric citrate
- 125ml (½ cup) cold water
- 12g (¼oz) potassium ferric cyanide
- 125ml (½ cup) cold water

2hrs ½hr

Spreading print

You will need

- Safety clothing
- Pins or tape
- Glass or plastic dye pots with lids for mixing and storing
- Electric hand-mixer or blender
- Glass or metal dye pots for mixing
- Clean wine-bottle cork
- Electric fan heater or hair dryer
- Small steamer and spatula

Ingredients

- 15g (½oz) starch ether
- 150ml (⅔ cup) warm water
- 10g (2tsp) ammonium oxalate
- 100ml (½ cup) hot water
- 5g (1tsp) acid dye powder colour
- 50ml (¼ cup) methylated spirits
- 25g (1oz) wetting agent
- 100ml (½ cup) cold water

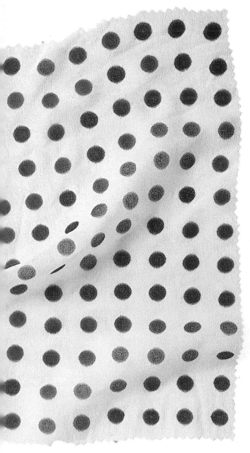

Block prints can be used to pattern silk fabric with simple yet effective shapes. This recipe uses a cork from a wine bottle to print the pattern onto the fabric. The stunning spreading effect on the fabric is created by adding methylated spirits to the dye paste.

1 Press the fabric well and, using pins or tape, attach it to your printing table (see page 30).

2 Wearing safety clothing, make the thickening binder into a paste by mixing the starch ether and 150ml (⅔ cup) warm water in a glass or plastic dye-mixing pot using an electric hand-mixer or blender.

3 Place 100ml (½ cup) of hot water in a glass or metal dye-mixing pot and add the ammonium oxalate, stirring to dissolve. Add the acid dye powder colour and stir well to dissolve thoroughly.

4 Add this dye solution to the thickening paste and stir in the methylated spirits, the wetting agent, and 100ml (½ cup) of cold water. Mix well until a smooth paste is formed.

5 Using a clean cork from a wine bottle, dab small amounts of the dye paste over the fabric to make a pattern, leaving enough room between each dab for the colour to spread out. Allow the paste to spread for 2 to 5 minutes and then dry the fabric with an electric fan heater or hair dryer.

6 These dyes now need to be fixed onto the fabric by steaming. Follow the instructions on page 25 and steam for 30 minutes.

7 After steaming, wash off carefully to avoid any unfixed dye staining undecorated areas. Rinse in plenty of cold running water and then wash in hand-hot water with a small amount of mild detergent. Finally, rinse in cold running water and leave to dry.

> **Testing acid dyes** Note that only certain acid dye powder colours will work with this recipe, so be sure to do a test first. You will also find that some colours will spread more quickly than others.

Stripping print

3hrs   10 mins   cotton

This recipe shows you how to create a stunning pattern on cotton by combining the techniques of colour stripping and block printing. A modern interpretation of traditional methods used for centuries in Asia, the recipe uses a printing block made of string, glue and varnish. Colour-stripping paste is then applied to the fabric using the block in a half-drop repeat.

1 Press the fabric well and using pins or tape, attach it to your printing table (see page 30).
2 Wearing safety clothing, make the thickening binder into a paste by mixing the modified guar gum and the 300ml (1⅓ cup) of warm water in a glass or plastic dye-mixing pot using an electric hand-mixer or blender.
3 In a glass or metal dye-mixing pot, dissolve the reducing agent in 100ml (½ cup) of hot water. Add the glycerine, stirring well to dissolve thoroughly.
4 Add the reducing agent solution to the thickening paste and stir well until a smooth paste is formed.
5 Pour a small amount of this mixture onto the sheet of glass or thick plastic and spread it out evenly with the rubber roller. Using the loaded roller, coat the ready-made cardboard block with the paste and then press the block firmly onto the fabric to print your pattern. Colour will be stripped away from these areas. Repeat this process until the fabric is patterned as you require. Leave to dry for about 1 to 2 hours, but not overnight as this will affect the results, making the stripped colour patchy.
6 The paste now needs to be fixed onto the fabric by steaming. Follow the instructions on page 25 and steam for 10 minutes.
7 After steaming, wash off carefully to avoid any paste staining undecorated areas. Rinse in cold running water and then in hand-hot water with a small amount of mild detergent. Finally, rinse in cold running water and leave to dry.

As with all dye-stripping recipes, this will only work on fabric which has been coloured with a dye which is suitable for the stripping process.

You will need

- Safety clothing
- Pins or tape
- Glass or plastic dye pots with lids for mixing and storing
- Electric hand-mixer or blender
- Glass or metal dye pots for mixing
- Ready-prepared cardboard printing block (see page 48)
- Sheet of glass or thick plastic
- Rubber roller and spatula
- Small steamer

Ingredients

- 40g (1½oz) modified guar gum
- 300ml (1⅓ cups) warm water
- 75g (2¾oz) sodium formaldehyde sulphoxylate (reducing agent)
- 25ml (5tsp) glycerine
- 100ml (½ cup) hot water

5 days   40°-80°C
(104°-176°F)

Organic block print

You will need

- Safety clothing
- Dye container
- Glass or metal dye pots for mixing
- Iron
- Glass or plastic dye pots with lids for mixing and storing
- Pins or tape and a spatula
- Block printing tool (see page 48)

Ingredients

- 7g (1½tsp) x 2 alum
- 7g (1½tsp) x 2 cream of tartar
- 150ml (⅔ cup) x 2 warm water
- 50–100ml (¼–½ cup) Madder liquid (see page 71)
- 100g (4oz) liquid gum arabic

Most natural dyes are applied to fabric in a dye container. However, you can also print or paint with some natural dyes, such as indigo, madder or cutch. Enough dye colour can be extracted from these plants to enable you to mix it with a simple binder, so that you can print or paint with these colours.

1 Wash your fabric in a mild detergent, rinse and dry.
2 Because you will use madder and cutch, you will need to mordant the fabric first. Mix up the mordant and follow the instructions on page 24.
3 Press the fabric well and, using pins or tape, attach it to your printing table (see page 30).
4 Wearing safety clothing, place the gum arabic in a glass or plastic dye-mixing pot and add the red madder liquid (made according to step 3 of the recipe on page 71) and mix together thoroughly.
5 Following the instructions on page 48, use the block printing tool to pattern your fabric. Leave to dry for 3 or 4 days.
6 Wearing safety clothing, mix together the second set of mordant ingredients following the instructions on page 24. This will further fix the natural madder paste into the fibres of the fabric.
7 Place the fabric in a dye container and add enough cold water to cover the fabric so that it can move freely under the water. Add the well-dissolved mordant mixture to the container. Slowly bring to the boil and simmer for 30 minutes.
8 Remove the fabric and rinse well under cold running water and then in warm water with a little mild detergent. Finally, rinse again in cold running water and leave to dry.

> **Alternative method** You can also use an after-mordant to add further variety to the colours you have printed by following the instructions on page 25.

Computer transfer

1hr   8-10 secs

This recipe shows you how to use a computer or colour copier to transfer a design to white fabric. The technique was developed as an alternative method for producing small production runs of individually designed T-shirts. You can use it to decorate a T-shirt, but it works equally well on other fabrics and garments.

You will need

- Computer ink-jet printer or colour copier
- Fabric-transfer paper or fabric colour copy paper
- Scissors
- Iron

1 Press the fabric well and, using pins or tape, attach it to your printing table (see page 30).
2 If using an ink-jet computer printer, print out your design onto fabric-transfer paper for an ink-jet printer. If you don't have an ink-jet printer, try a copier shop – many stock fabric-transfer paper and will transfer the design for you. In either case, remember to print your design out as a mirror image as it is transferred face down onto your fabric. If you are using a fine fabric, a design of small, individual shapes that can be cut out and transferred individually works best, because a large design will affect the handling quality of the fabric.
3 Cut out the transfer design and place face-down on your fabric. Using a hot iron, iron over the paper, pressing firmly for 8 to 10 seconds to transfer the design. Check if it has transferred by lifting a corner of the paper slightly. If necessary, iron for a few seconds longer. While still hot, peel the backing paper completely away from the fabric in one quick movement to reveal your design.

> A number of different types of fabric-transfer papers for different applications are available, such as paper for transferring designs onto a black fabric. Do be sure to try something other than a T-shirt!

cotton

linen

silk

wool

nylon

viscose

polyester

mixed fibres

1 day

Rust patterning

You will need
- Safety clothing
- Dye container
- Glass dye pots for mixing

Ingredients
- 20ml (4tsp) acid acetic 80% tech
- 100ml (½ cup) cold water
- 250g (9oz) iron filings

Although rust stains on fabric are usually to be avoided, you can obtain some unusual colour shades and intriguing patterns by scattering iron filings on silk.

1 Wash the fabric with a mild detergent to remove any surface finishes so that the dye can take evenly across the whole piece. Leave to dry.
2 Wearing safety clothing, place the cold water in a glass dye-mixing pot and add the acetic acid. Always add acid to water, never water to acid. Add the iron filings to the acetic acid solution and leave to soak overnight.
3 Using pins or tape, attach your fabric to your printing table (see page 30). Wearing safety clothing, carefully remove the iron filings from the acetic acid solution and, taking care not to handle the fabric too much, scatter the damp iron filings over your fabric to form a random pattern. Leave for 1 to 2 hours.
4 Carefully lift off all the iron filings from the fabric and then rinse in warm water with a small amount of mild detergent. Finally, rinse in cold water and leave to dry.

> **Alternative colourway** Try experimenting with this recipe by leaving the iron filings on the fabric for different lengths of time to produce different depths of colour.

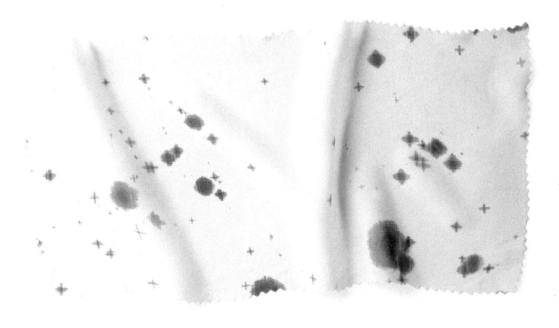

Flour paste resist

4 hrs   30°–80°C
(86°–176°F)

cotton

Asia has perhaps the longest history of resist-dyed fabrics, with superb samples still surviving that date back several thousand years. Today the paste-resist technique is still widely used throughout the world to decorate fabrics. The cassava paste detailed in this recipe is still used by the Yoruba people of Nigeria.

1 Press the fabric well and, using pins or tape, attach it to your printing table (see page 30).

2 Wearing safety clothing, mix the flour paste resist using either the plain flour recipe or the cassava flour recipe. To make the plain flour resist, mix the cold water and flour in a glass or metal dye-mixing pot, stirring well. Heat the mixture on an electric or gas ring, stirring continuously until a thick paste is formed. Allow to cool slightly, then carefully stir in the liquid gum arabic. To make the cassava flour resist, mix the hot water and cassava flour in a glass or metal dye-mixing pot, stirring well. Heat on an electric or gas ring, stirring continuously for 20 to 30 minutes until a paste is formed. Leave to cool and then strain.

3 Using the block printing tool and pad, decorate the fabric with the paste to form your design (see page 48). Leave to dry thoroughly.

4 Using the indigo dye recipe on page 72, dip the patterned fabric in the vat to colour the fabric and then leave to dry in the air to oxidize. Finally wash the fabric as described in the indigo recipe.

You will need

- Safety clothing
- Pins or tape
- Glass or metal dye pots for mixing
- Spatula
- Dye container
- Strainer
- Block printing tool and pad (see page 48)
- Indigo dye (see page 72)

Ingredients

- 150g (5½oz) plain cooking flour
- 200ml (¾ cup) cold water
- 150ml (⅔ cup) liquid gum arabic

or

- 125g (4½oz) cassava flour
- 300ml (1½ cups) hot water

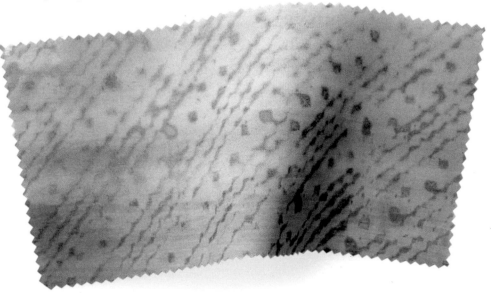

4 hrs   10 mins

Roller stripping

You will need

- Safety clothing
- Pins or tape
- Glass or plastic dye pots with lids for mixing and storing
- Electric hand-mixer or blender
- Glass or metal dye pots for mixing
- Rubber roller and spatula
- Sheet of glass or thick plastic
- Small steamer

Ingredients

- 30g (1½oz) modified guar gum
- 250ml (1 cup) warm water
- 25g (1oz) urea
- 100ml (½ cup) hot water
- 100g (4oz) zinc formaldehyde sulphoxylate (reducing agent)
- 20ml (4tsp) glycerine
- 10ml (2tsp) wetting agent

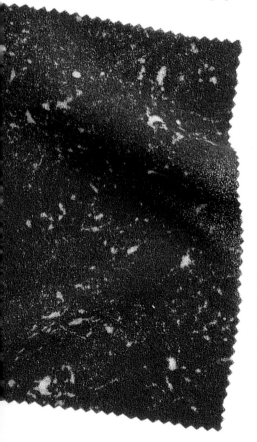

This recipe shows you how to create an interesting tonal effect on wool by taking away the colour using a simple decorator's rubber roller. By working the roller over and over the fabric, putting more or less paste in selected areas, an intriguing build-up of pattern will emerge.

1 Press the fabric well and, using pins or tape, attach it to your printing table (see page 30).

2 Wearing safety clothing, make the thickening binder into a paste by mixing the modified guar gum with 250ml (1 cup) warm water in a glass or plastic dye-mixing pot using an electric hand-mixer or blender.

3 In a glass or metal dye-mixing pot, dissolve the urea in 100ml (½ cup) of hot water.

4 Add the dissolved urea solution to the thickening paste, and then add the reducing agent, glycerine, and wetting agent. Stir thoroughly, or mix with an electric hand-mixer or blender, until a smooth paste is formed.

5 Now use a roller to pattern your fabric. First pour a small amount of the paste onto the glass or plastic sheet and spread it out evenly across the sheet with the roller. Run the loaded roller across the fabric – by reloading it and criss-crossing across the fabric, you can vary the amount of paste over the fabric and form a pattern. Leave to dry for 1 to 2 hours, but not overnight as this will affect the results.

6 Follow the instructions for steaming on page 25 and steam for 10 minutes. After steaming, the colour will be stripped away from the decorated areas.

7 After steaming, wash off carefully. Rinse in plenty of cold running water. Then wash in hand-hot water with a small amount of mild detergent. Finally, rinse in cold running water and leave to dry.

Alternative method You can add 5g (1tsp) of zinc oxide to the paste in step 4 if you find that the colour is not stripping away fully. However, this can leave a stiff residue if not fully washed off in stage 7.

As with all dye-stripping recipes, this will only work on fabric which has been coloured with a dye which is suitable for the stripping process.

Illuminated block-printing

4 hrs   10 mins   silk

wool

Ready-made block-printing pads for interior decorating use can also be used on fabrics. The range and scale of designs are particularly suitable for printing borders. In this recipe, block prints are used to create a border pattern with one illuminating colour.

1 Press the fabric well and, using pins or tape, attach it to your printing table (see page 30).

2 Wearing safety clothing, make the thickening binder into a paste by mixing the modified guar gum with 250ml (1 cup) of warm water in a glass or plastic dye-mixing pot using an electric hand-mixer or blender.

3 In a glass or metal dye-mixing pot, dissolve the urea in 100ml (½ cup) of hot water and stir well. Add the illuminating dye powder colour and the glycerine and stir well to dissolve any lumps.

4 Add this solution to the thickening paste and mix well. Add in the reducing agent and wetting agent, and stir well to form a smooth paste .

5 Do this for each of the colours required. These dye paste colours will last a few days in airtight containers.

6 Pour a small amount of the dye paste onto the block-printing pad and allow the paste to soak into the pad for 1 to 2 minutes. Dab the block-printing tool onto the pad to pick up the paste and apply to the fabric to form your pattern. Allow each colour to dry before applying the next. Leave to dry for 1 to 2 hours, but not overnight as this will affect the results. Colour will be stripped away from the patterned areas to reveal a new colour.

7 These dyes now need to be fixed onto the fabric by steaming. Follow the instructions on page 25 and steam for 10 minutes.

8 After steaming, wash off carefully. Wash in warm water containing the hydrogen peroxide to develop the colours fully on your fabric. Then wash in warm water with mild detergent, rinse in cold water and leave to dry.

You will need
- Safety clothing
- Pins or tape
- Glass or plastic dye pots with lids for mixing and storing
- Electric hand-mixer or blender
- Glass or metal dye pots for mixing
- Ready-to-use block print (see page 48)
- Block print pad (see page 48)
- Small steamer and spatula

Ingredients
- 30g (1½oz) modified guar gum
- 250ml (1 cup) warm water
- 15g (½oz) urea
- 100ml (½cup) hot water
- 5g (1tsp) illuminating dye powder colour
- 25ml (5tsp) glycerine
- 100g (4oz) sodium formaldehyde sulphoxylate (reducing agent)
- 10ml (2tsp) wetting agent
- 5ml (1tsp) hydrogen peroxide

1 day   45 mins

Crackle effect

You will need
- Safety clothing
- Pins or tape
- Glass or metal dye pots for mixing
- Decorator's paintbrush and spatula
- Blank silkscreen (see page 50)
- Squeegee
- Iron
- Small steamer

Ingredients
- 250g (9oz) corn or potato dextrin powder
- 250ml (1 cup) boiling water
- Acid dye paste (see page 119)

A different type of resist pattern can be obtained by using either corn or potato dextrin. A crackled effect is left on the fabric from the dextrin resist after painting a fabric dye over the surface of the fabric. The recipe is used here on a fine wool fabric.

1 Press the fabric well and, using pins or tape, attach it to your printing table (see page 30).
2 Wearing safety clothing, place the boiling water in a glass or metal dye-mixing pot and add the dextrin powder, stirring thoroughly to mix. Heat on an electric or gas ring and simmer for 10 to 15 minutes, stirring constantly to form a smooth paste. Leave to cool.
3 Using the decorator's paintbrush, apply the dextrin paste all over the fabric. Leave to dry overnight to allow the fine crackle lines to form on the fabric. For thicker crackle lines, dry the paste with an electric fan heater or hair dryer.
4 Following the instructions for the recipe on page 119 using acid dyes, mix up a colour to screenprint over your prepared fabric.
5 Using the blank silkscreen and squeegee, pull the acid dye across the fabric with the squeegee 2 or 3 times. Wash the screen and squeegee immediately. Leave the fabric to dry.
6 Now fix the dyes onto the fabric by steaming. Follow the instructions on page 25 and steam for 45 minutes.
7 After steaming, wash off carefully to avoid any unfixed dye staining undecorated areas. Rinse in plenty of cold running water and then wash in hand-hot water with a small amount of mild detergent. Finally, rinse in cold running water and leave to dry.

Alternative method You can use this technique on other fabric types simply by using the appropriate dyestuff for the base fabric used.

Glossary

These are the main chemicals and binders that are used throughout the book. While many of them have complex technical names their functions in the recipes are quite straightforward: helping the dyes to colour and stay on the fabric.

Thickeners

These are the main thickening binders used in the book as carriers for the dye colours and chemicals needed in the painting and printing recipes.

Carageenan seaweed extract used in marbling

Glitter binder used on all fabric types

Metallic pigment binder used on all fabric types.

Modified guar gum used on wool and silk for devoré and discharge techniques

Modified starch used in vat and devoré techniques

Neutral pigment binder used on all fabric types

Opaque pigment binder used on all fabric types

Sodium alginate thickener used on cotton, linen, viscose and silk

Dyeing assistants

These are the main dyeing and decorating assistants used in the recipes to help the dye colours fix onto and penetrate the fabric and yarn.

VAT DYEING ASSISTANTS
Assistants for natural dyeing (mordant auxiliaries)
Potassium aluminium sulphate
Potassium hydrogen tartrate

Assistants for synthetic dyeing (fixing auxiliaries)
Acetic acid
Formic acid
Household salt
Polyester dye carrier

PAINTING AND PRINTING PASTE ASSISTANTS
Sodium hydroxide mercerizes and burns away protein fibres, eg wool or silk

Urea solvent and hygroscopic agent used to attract moisture during the steaming process

Glycerine solvent and hygroscopic agent used to attract moisture during the steaming process

Perminal KB wetting agent

Zinc formaldehyde sulphoxylate reducing agent

Sodium formaldehyde sulphoxylate reducing agent

Liquid gum arabic glue

Aluminium sulphate mordant, also burns away cellulose fibres eg in devoré techniques

Resist salt L oxidising agent

Calgon water softener (brand name)

Ammonium oxalate/ammonium sulphate acid generator

Sodium carbonate/sodium bicarbonate alkali and fixing auxiliaries

Suppliers

UK

Ashill Colour Studio
Boundary Cottage
172 Clifton Road
Shefford
Bedfordshire SC17 5AH
Natural dyes, mordants, books

Candlemakers Suppliers
28 Blythe Road
London W14 0HA
Tel 020-7602 4031
Dyes, waxes, equipment

Clariant
Claverley Lane
Horsforth
Leeds LS18 4RD
Tel 0113-258 4646
Dyes and dyeing chemicals

Fairfield Yarns
Office
9 Lea Mount Drive
Fairfield
Bury
Lancahire BL9 7RR
Tel 0161-797 8349
Millshop and warehouse
131 Rochdale Road East
Heywood
Lancashire OL10 1QU
Tel 01706-623808
www.fairfieldyarns.co.ukyarns

Fibrecrafts
Style Cottage
Lower Eashing
Godalming
Surrey GU7 2QD
Tel 01483-565800
Natural dyes, mordants

Handweavers Studio and Gallery
29 Haroldstone Road
Lodon E17 7AN
Tel 020-8521 2281
www.geocities.com/athens/agora/9814
Yarns

Midland Dykem
71 Paget Road
Leicester LE3 5HN
Tel 0116-2624975
Dyes and chemicals sold in a minimum quantity of 1kg (34oz), but reasonably priced and a good selection

Pongees
28 Hoxton Square
London N1 6NN
Tel 020-7739 9130
Undyed silk

Quality Colours (London) Ltd
Unit 13
Landmann Way
London SE14 5RL
Tel 020-7394 8775
Pigment binders and colours, modified guar gum, sodium alginate thickener and other chemicals needed for dyeing

Ronald Britton & Company
Unit 1
Kingsway West Business Park
Moss Bridge Road
Rochdale
Lancashire
Tel 01707-643761
Glitter powder

CSL
Jaycee House
Croydon Business Centre
214 Purley Way
Croydon
Surrey CR0 4XG
Tel 020 8256 1500
Silkscreens, squeegees, coatings for silkscreens

Suasion
35 Riding House Street
London W1P 7PT
Tel 020-7580 3763
Dyes and dyeing chemicals sold in small quantities

Texere Yarns
College Mill
Barkerend Road
Bradford
West Yorkshire BD1 4AU
Tel 01274-722191
www.texere-yarns.co.uk
Undyed yarn

The Magic Touch
Unit 4
Apex Business Centre
Boscombe Road
Dunstable
Bedfordshire LU5 4SB
Tel 01582-671444
Transfer paper for photocopier or computer printer

Thomas & Vines Ltd.
Units 5 & 6
Sutherland Court
Tolpits Lane
Watford
Herts WD1 8SP
Tel 01923-775111

Flocking gun hire, flocking
powder, flocking glue

Tiranti
27 Warren Street
London W1P 5DG
Tel 020-7636 8565
Latex

Whaleys (Bradford) Ltd
Harris Court
Great Horton
Bradford

West Yorkshire BD7 4E8
Tel 01274-576718
All types of undyed fabric

Wolfin Textiles Ltd
64 Great Titchfield Street
London W1P 7AE
Tel 020-7636 4949
Undyed cotton

Yeoman Yarns
36 Churchill Way
Fleckney
Leicestershire LE8 8UD
Tel 0116-240 4464
www.yeomanyarns.co.uk
Undyed yarn

Canada and United States

Aljo Manufacturing Ltd
81-83 Franklin St
New York
NY 10013
212 226 2878
Synthetic dyes, batik materials

Colorado Wholesale Dye Corp
2139 S. Sheridan Blvd
Denver
CO 80227
1 800 697 1566
www.bestdye.com
Dyes for cotton, linen, silk

Dharma Trading Co.
PO Box 150916
San Rafael
CA 94915
800 542 5227
www.dharmatrading.com
Most dye supplies

Earth Guild
33 Haywood Street
Asheville
NC 28801

1800 327 8448
www.earthguild.com
Natural dyes

G&S Dye
250 Dundas St W. #8
Toronto
ON M5T 2Z5
416 596 0550
www.gsdye.com
Most dye supplies

Hagenon Laboratories
1302 Washingotn
Manitowoc
W1 54220
920 683 3339
Chemicals

Janlynn Corporation
34 Front St
PO Box 51848
Indian Orchard
MA 01151–5848
413 543 7500
www.janlynn.com
Most dye supplies

Jaquard Products
PO Box 425
Healdsburg
CA 95448
1800 422 0455
www.jacquardproducts.com
Synthetic dyes and chemicals

Maiwa Handprints Ltd
6-1666 Johnston Street
Granville Island
Vancouver
BC V6H 3S2
604 669 3939
www.maiwa.com
Natural dyes

PRO Chemical and Dye
994 Jefferson St
Fall River
MA 02726
1800 228 9393
www.prochemical.com
Synthetic dyes and chemicals

Index

Bibliography

Dye Plants and Dyeing
John and Margaret Cannon
UK, Herbert Press
1 87156 974 5

Exploring Fabric Printing
Stuart and Patricia Robinson
US, Charles T. Brantford (1971)
0 82317 021 7

Fabric Dyeing and Printing
Kate Wells
UK, Conran Octopus (1997)
1 84091 145 X
US, Interweave Press
1 88301 035 7

Indigo Textiles: Technique and History
Gosta Sandberg
US, Lark books (1989)
0 93727 440 2

Manual of Dyes and Fabric
Joyce Storey
UK, Thames & Hudson (reprint 1992)
0 50068 016 7

Natural Dyeing without Chemicals
Jenny Dean
UK, J Dean (1996)
0 95308 350 0

Natural Dyes, Fast or Fugitive
Gill Dalby
UK, Haldanes Craft & Tools (1994)
0 95252 740 5

Shibori: the Art of Fabric Folding, Pleating and Dyeing
Elfriede Moëller
UK & US, Search Press (1999)
0 85532 895 9

Wild Colour
Jenny Dean
UK, Mitchell Beazley (1999)
1 84000 084 8
US, Watson-Guptill (Wild Color)
0 82305 727 5

Author Acknowledgements
The author would like to thank Wendy Wilson for the rowan blueprinting sample and Judith Selton for marbling samples. Thanks also to Rosie, Sharon and all my family, friends and students for all their help and encouragement